Sophie's Kiss

Sophie's Kiss

The true love story of Prince Edward
and Sophie Rhys-Jones

Garth Gibbs and Sean Smith

BLAKE

Published by Blake Publishing Ltd,
3 Bramber Court, 2 Bramber Road, London W14 9PB, England

First published in paperback in Great Britain in 1999

ISBN 1 85782 3729

British Library Cataloguing-in-Publication Data:
A catalogue record for this book is available from the British
Library.

Typeset by BCP

Printed in Great Britain by
Creative Print and Design (Wales), Ebbw Vale, Gwent.

3 5 7 9 10 8 6 4 2

Photos reproduced by kind permission of
All Action, News International, Press Association,
Rex Features, UK Press, Glenn Harvey.

Acknowledgements

Writing this book has been a curious mixture of open and shut doors. The couple themselves, who are shy about their relationship, would probably have preferred nothing to have been written about their love story, but they should be consoled by the fact that, without exception, everyone who helped with this book wishes them well. Although Prince Edward is used to featuring in books, it will be a new experience for Sophie Rhys-Jones and we sincerely hope it is not a painful one.

Considerable thanks are due to Margaret Holder for her invaluable research and expert advice. We have quoted from, and are grateful to, the following books: *Prince Edward, A Biography* by Ingrid Seward; *Prince Edward, A Life in the Spotlight* by Paul James; *Commando, Survival of the Fittest* by Robin Eggar; *Diana's Nightmare, The Family* by Chris Hutchins and Peter Thompson. Thanks also to author Andrew Morton for revealing the romance in the first place and keeping us abreast of developments in a number of excellent articles.

A final thanks to the people who have helped, notably Janie Stewart, Brian MacLaurin, Leanne Tritton-Jones, Nick Skeens, Peter Brown, Neil Fox, Graham Dene, Marino Franchi, Andrew Parkinson, Mike Whitehill, Jayne Fincher, Judy Wade, Gareth Crump, Warren Gibbs, Alice de Smith, Andrew Murray, Tim and Eileen Graham, Trevor Vickery, Alison Jane Reid, Zoë Lawrence and many others, including those friendly people in the pubs around Sophie's home village of Brenchley.

*To every girl
who has ever dreamed of becoming a princess ...*

Contents

Preface

Breaking the Royal Mould

Listing everything we knew about Sophie Rhys-Jones before writing this book took rather less time than it takes to write a short shopping list. We had read that she works in public relations but keeps a low profile. We thought of her as the type of girl we might see at a Point to Point meeting in the country. In photographs she appears attractive and natural rather than stunning. She resembles a petite version of BBC presenter Jill Dando. And that's about all there was. In effect, *Sophie's Kiss* began life as a blank canvas.

Even though Sophie has been the girlfriend of the Queen's youngest son for more than five years, she has managed to slip relatively unnoticed into the Royal world. The British public and the media have understandably focused on the Duchess of York and the late Princess of Wales. It still seems incredible, however, that the next Royal princess should have escaped intense public scrutiny. So far Sophie and

Edward have kept their heads well below the parapets of Windsor Castle and, as a result, have enjoyed a luxury of privacy denied to Diana and Fergie. The only time they seem to be pictured together is when they arrive for someone else's wedding. After their wedding day on 19 June, only time will tell how their married life develops.

Sophie has survived thus far with her dignity intact. Our fears that this might be because she was rather boring and had never done anything interesting proved to be wide of the mark. It soon became apparent that Sophie is a girl blessed with the spirit of adventure. Her royal motto should be *carpe diem*, because she certainly 'seizes the day'. She has grabbed her chance to fulfil a dream — with both hands steady as a rock.

Sophie was born in 1965 when The Beatles and The Rolling Stones were fashioning their legends, and Harold Wilson was puffing on his pipe at Number Ten. The 'swinging sixties' passed by the sleepy Kent village of Brenchley, barely causing a ripple in Sophie's happy childhood. Her parents were of the typically English type who believed that education was a better indicator of class than money, and they stretched themselves to provide the best schooling possible for Sophie and her elder brother David. It is an investment that has paid high dividends because Sophie has the social tools to, as her former employer Brian MacLaurin observed, 'charm the birds from the trees'. Sophie has always been a popular girl who could be relied upon to be fun.

It is, however, her adventurous streak that makes Sophie stand out from the Royal crowd. Even though she had a solid and enjoyable job at Capital Radio, she left to become a ski rep at a Swiss resort and then, instead of returning to London, she travelled to the other side of the world with her Australian boyfriend.

When that did not work out she stayed on to work and travel, instead of running home with her tail between her legs. This, we discovered, was a girl with true grit. By the time Sophie met Edward, she was an independent, mature, well-travelled young woman light years ahead of Diana and Fergie in terms of their emotional maturity when they first became involved in the World of the Windsors. Sophie has needed all of that maturity to stay with Edward thoughout the controversy and sadness which have beset the Royal Family these past few years. Edward himself could not be further from a conventional royal prince. He is neither playboy nor prude, nor is he some sort of ultimate Hooray Henry figure. He is a man of sensitivity, ambition and inner strength. He and Sophie share many interests and where they did not, she made the effort to bridge the gap by learning to shoot, improving her riding skills and trying her hand at windsurfing in the chilly waters of the Solent. She shares a 'have a go' enthusiasm with Edward, which he much admires. And let's not forget, she is in love.

Since they first started getting serious about one another in late 1993 they have been subjected to endless speculation as to when they might get married. Royal author Andrew Morton, who first told the world about the romance, bet £10 that they would marry within a year. The bookies William Hill refused to take any more bets. On a visit to Africa just after he had met Sophie the Prince was told by the President of Ghana: 'I hope when you return you will come back with a wife.' Edward cheerily replied that he would see what he could do. Since then at Christmas and New Year there has been firm and definite news in the press that the couple would be announcing their engagement shortly. But it never happened. Although we discovered they were planning to announce their engagement three years ago, the fact is that they just have not had the opportunity to get married. The very public crumbling of Charles' and Andrew's marriages left Edward and Sophie in an impossible position. And then the unthinkable happened on 31 August 1997 when Princess Diana was tragically killed and the whole world mourned. Both Edward and Sophie realised that it would take time for the country to be ready to accept a new royal marriage.

Towards the end of 1998, the 50th birthday celebrations of Prince Charles and the gradual emergence into the spotlight of his sons William and Harry were the first steps on the ladder of the Royal Family being re-established in the affections of the public. Edward and Sophie wanted to be sure that their love was not used to bribe the nation to like the Royals. They do not want to be acclaimed as the saviours of the Royal Family. It is a suggestion that makes their blood boil with anger. They do not believe the monarchy needs saving and they certainly do not think it is fair to place such a burden on their marriage.

Sophie and Edward clearly have a partnership that has broken the Royal mould of relationships. They both have independent careers heading their own increasingly successful companies. They share their lives in a thoroughly relaxed and modern manner. They have the busy, comfortable lifestyle of t.wo independent, privileged, well-off people. Sophie already enjoys many of the trappings of royalty and is treated like a princess when she goes to a function. This is something that photographer Jayne Fincher has noticed more and more in the last year or two. Sophie can come and go at Buckingham Palace as she pleases. She joins Edward for country weekends at some of the most beautiful houses in the land. The Queen and Prince Philip like her and, at the end of the day, that is the most important thing within Royal circles. It is a dream life for an ordinary girl from a small Kent village. Sophie is by no means a Cinderella and Edward is no Prince Charming, but it is inspiring that they have made their relationship work in unlikely, even unpromising, circumstances. The announcement of their engagement on a sunny January morning was the best news for the Royal family for years. Already, Sophie is coming to terms with a media feeding frenzy. She is accompanied on her morning walk from Buckingham Palace to her Mayfair offices by a group of picture-hungry photographers. On her 34th birthday on 20 January, she was presented with a huge bouquet of flowers by a reporter from the *Sun* newspaper.

She is having to bear the inevitable comparisons with the Princess of Wales and, like Diana, is having to make decisions that will affect the rest of her life — not least deciding on whether to have a full-time Royal bodyguard or not. Through all this attention Sophie's smile has never left her face and she appears to be walking on air. When asked by a journalist how things were going, she replied simply, 'Engaged life is rather nice.'

Part One

1

The Witches of Cranbrook

Rumour has it that, on her Royal progress through Kent, Queen Elizabeth I spent the night at the building that now houses the Dulwich College Preparatory School in the village of Cranbrook, about ten miles from that favourite London commuter spot Tunbridge Wells. A century or so later and a few miles away, the beautiful village of Brenchley became home to one of the most famous Royal mistresses, Nell Gwynne. King Charles II installed her in the Old Palace — a collection of sprawling, gabled, half-timbered buildings with an overhanging upper storey. She bore his illegitimate son but became jealous and distressed when the King, who had acknowledged many of his other illegitimate children, hesitated in recognising this latest offspring. On one glorious summer's day he is reputed to have paid a call to his dear Nellie and was most surprised by the greeting he received. According to legend, instead of a welcome, Nell Gwynne held their baby son out of the window and threatened to drop him into the murky depths of the moat below. The King heaved a weary sigh and just in time issued the laconic command, 'Don't let the Duke of St Albans drown.' And so it was that another bastard became a member of the British aristocracy. Some years later the Old Palace became the home of the first Duke of St Albans and remained privately owned until it was sold to the local council after the Second World War.

Although Princess Anne went to school at nearby Benenden there has been little Royal progress in this backwater of Kent since those Restoration times — and not much rumour either. However, that has all changed since Sophie Rhys-Jones blew into the House of Windsor like a cooling breeze. As a child Sophie was like the quintessential Enid Blyton heroine of the classic *Mallory Towers* boarding-school books for girls. Brought up in a beautiful part of the English countryside, she was popular with teachers and girls, had lovely, supportive parents and was brilliant at games. Nevertheless, even Enid Blyton herself might have baulked at Sophie falling in love with a charming prince. It is a world where fantasy has merged into reality.

Sophie Helen Rhys-Jones was born at the Nuffield Maternity Home in Oxford on 20 January, 1965, just four days before the nation went into mourning following the death of Winston Churchill. She was given the name Helen in memory of her father's sister who had been tragically killed in a riding accident more than ten years earlier. At the time of her birth her father Christopher, mother Mary and elder brother David lived in the village of Ickford in Buckinghamshire, but shortly after Sophie was born they moved to Brenchley, which has since remained the family home. Mr Rhys-Jones, who placed the hyphen in the family surname, was an overseas representative for a car manufacturer and it made sense for him to live near Dover and Folkestone because of his frequent trips to the continent.

After a couple of years in a small house in the centre of the village they moved to the quaintly named 'Homestead Farmhouse', a very comfortable four-bedroom 17th-century thatched farmhouse on the edge of Brenchley — at today's prices it would probably fetch £200,000. It is a typical weather-boarded Kent house with whitewashed walls and bits of buildings stuck on the side, almost as an afterthought. In winter a large pile of logs is crammed into the sun porch at the back. Inside, the rooms are furnished comfortably with simple wooden furniture covered in faded chintz material. Pride of place is given to an old Welsh dresser adorned with brightly coloured plates. One of the house's best features, which is even more important now considering all the publicity that the family has attracted, is that it is difficult to spot from the road, being tucked away at the end of a footpath. The view from all four bedrooms is quite inspiring and reaches across acres of trees and rolling fields. Homestead Farmhouse has offered Sophie a happy and secure environment, one which she appreciates most keenly when her busy lifestyle allows her to escape to the calm of Brenchley.

Her father, Christopher, had a tenuous link with the gossip columns even before his daughter's supersonic flight into society's stratosphere. As a holiday job in his late teens he once taught the *Daily Mail*'s renowned diarist Nigel Dempster at his parents' prep school at Lympstone in Devon. Until he finally settled in Kent, Christopher had led quite a nomadic life. He had been born in Sarawak, Borneo, but his father Theo returned home to be headmaster of St Peter's prep school at Lympstone — later the scene of Prince Edward's unhappy experience in the Marines. When he left Kings Bruton School, a respectable boys' public school in nearby Somerset, he spent a lot of time travelling in Africa before settling on a career. He and his wife Mary soon became popular in Brenchley where they were considered very sociable by all and sundry. Local farmer and friend Michael Noakes, whose family have farmed in and around the Brenchley area for five generations says: 'We always tease people that you have to be here for 25 years before you are accepted. But this is not so. If you come here and mix easily you are accepted straight away. Christopher and Mary were popular pretty early on.' Christopher's enjoyment of outdoor pursuits like sailing, shooting and fishing and his love of nature had a lasting effect on his daughter — as a little girl she would don a pair of wellington boots and happily tag along with her father. He also enjoys the indoor pursuit of a good gin and tonic, which has always been *de rigueur* in Brenchley society. Years later when Sophie dropped the bombshell that she was going out with Prince Edward, her father memorably remarked: 'It was the first time in my life that I needed a gin and tonic before 10 o'clock.'

Christopher met his wife-to-be Mary O'Sullivan, a bank manager's daughter, on a trip to Gibraltar. She was working as a secretary in South Kensington and living on Sloane Avenue, so in some ways she was an original Sloane Ranger — a trail that Sophie was to follow when she left school. In fact, Sophie is not the first member of the Rhys-Jones family to come into close contact with a prince. Her mother once danced with a dashing Prince Philip at a society ball. When Christopher and Mary moved to Kent they were determined to do their very best for their children. They worked hard to find the money to pay for private schooling for Sophie and her brother David who is two years older. For many years Mary worked as a secretary for Lambert and Foster, an estate agent in nearby Paddock Wood. To make some extra pennies she also advertised her secretarial skills locally, offering to type reports, letters, theses, CVs and book manuscripts and this work made all the difference to the family's finances. It also meant that she was available to run the children to and from school. Sophie's childhood friend Janie Stewart, whose father was a local vet, says of Mary Rhys-Jones: 'I remember her as being a proper "Mum" figure. She would always have chocolate biscuits in the house.'

Sophie and David went to the Dulwich College Preparatory School in Cranbrook, about nine miles from Brenchley along typically high-hedged Kent lanes. The prep school had been separated from the famous London public school when the pupils were evacuated during the Second World War. After the War the older pupils moved back to the main school but the juniors remained in Cranbrook. Sophie was four years and nine months old when she started at the junior part of the school, called Nash House. The fee for each term was £29.7s, which in pre-decimal days was quite a tidy sum. A big circular driveway led up to the school and was clogged every morning with Volvos dropping little ones off at Nash House.

Sophie usually travelled to school with a girl called Joanna Patterson who also lived in Brenchley. Sophie was in a class of 20 boys and girls, split up into little groups according to their activity that day. When the children arrived at school each day, they were sent out to the playground, an open field that was quite the biggest young Sophie had ever seen. At one end there was a sand pit and some tree houses and climbing equipment, which Sophie loved. Janie Stewart remembers: 'Basically we would meet up with all our friends and play. We would go out and run around and fight the nasty little boys. After that we would be called in for a drink of milk in those quarter bottles with straws, which was quite disgusting. We sort of had lessons, counting and stories like Brer Rabbit. In the afternoon we would have a story and then we could either play quietly or we could lie down on one of the camp beds and have a nap. It was nice having a kip in the afternoon. Sophie was quite a good little girl, but she was easily led by the naughtier girls — for example, when we had a rebellion and locked ourselves in the Wendy House. We shouted that we weren't coming out. It was a proper house with a lock on the door and three children could get into it together. After that it became quite a problem with children locking themselves in the Wendy House so they had to take the door off.'

Although Sophie and her friends were very young, they spent the entire day at Nash House. It was considered a proper school and discipline was quite strict. If a boy or girl was naughty, they had to stand in the corner with their face turned to the wall which must be frightening for a small person. At an early age Sophie decided this was not for her and punishment was a dish best avoided. As a result she had a happy knack of escaping at just the right time leaving her friends to face the music. It was also at this time that Sophie developed her lifelong love of water. In summer all the children would jump into the kiddies' pool and splash around until it was decided that they could swim properly. Then they were given a swimming costume and cap and were allowed to go down to the big pool with the older children. It was a step that everyone was keen to take and Sophie was the first in her year to get a costume. Since then, she has always excelled at swimming.

At the age of seven Sophie moved on to the next stage at school when the girls and the 'nasty little boys' were split up. The girls moved to a building called 'Little Stream' and had to wear a school uniform, which, as all parents know, is a major hidden expense. Sophie's clothing list was a typical one: navy raincoat, grey felt hat with hat band, grey school blazer, tunic, blue jersey (school colour), blue blouse (school colour), grey knickers, grey knee-length socks, brown walking shoes (lace-ups) and two overalls. In winter she needed a pair of grey woollen gloves, school scarf (optional) and a navy duffel coat with red lining (optional). For the summer term she had to have a school summer dress and knickers, school cardigan and white ankle socks. Everything had to be bought from Simmonds and Son, the school outfitters in Calverley Road, Tunbridge Wells. Mary Rhys-Jones, who had been taking in extra typing to meet this expense, took Sophie along to the shop to get her kitted out. Sophie could never understand why she could not wear jeans to school. Her mother's work was not yet done because when they returned home she had the tedious task of sewing a name tag saying 'S. Rhys-Jones' into every single item. The other drawback to Sophie moving to Little Stream was that the fees were increased to £95 per term.

Sophie's special gang at this time comprised Janie Stewart, Sophie Douglas and Tracy Foreman, whose home in the village of Headcorn the others loved to visit because her wealthy parents kept horses and the girls, as girls do, would hang around the stables making nuisances of themselves. They also enjoyed watching Janie's father at work in his surgery treating cats, dogs and hamsters. The girls would stay over at each others' houses, which Sophie always looked forward to because it meant there would be a midnight feast. It had to be midnight and the girls had to wake up even if they were fast asleep. Each feast was planned like a military exercise with the girls tiptoeing downstairs to raid the larder and sneak back to the bedroom armed with goodies like Coca Cola, crisps and chocolate biscuits. The mothers, who were not supposed to know what was going on, always made sure they got in extra supplies. Sophie's mother, who was very jolly and down to earth, always found these furtive feasts highly entertaining.

Summer was a magical time in rural Kent. When they mowed the grass of the school playing-field Sophie and her gang would make a camp from grass cuttings. Then they would lay out a show-jumping course for themselves and pretend it was Hickstead. Their summer dresses had little bow-ties at the back, which they untied and pretended were reins so that they could play 'ponies'. The girls would charge around the field shouting 'whoa' and making clip-clop noises. It was an age of wonderful innocence. Horses were definitely the goal in life for the girls and, sadly, Sophie was the only one of the four friends who never had a pony. There was a very competitive streak in the 'horsy' world and, without a pony, Sophie was stuck on a lower social rung. As a result she has never been much of a rider, preferring to stride around the countryside on her own two feet than see it from the back of a strapping hunter. She would also join her friends cycling around the country lanes in a sheltered age, not too long ago, when it was considered safe to do so. At this stage of their lives Sophie and her friends had very little contact with boys, apart from seeing them across the field playing rugby or cricket while they played hockey and lacrosse.

Sophie was quite tall for her age and slim with light brown hair, which turned blonder under the summer sun. Her hair was longer than her now familiar bob and would always be tied back for school. That was compulsory, and any girl who decided she would wear her hair loose would find herself sitting outside the headmaster's study. That never happened to Sophie. 'She wasn't exactly a goody-goody but she was definitely a nice girl that everybody liked,' recalls Janie Stewart. 'She wasn't really rebellious like the other three of us might have been. She would toe the line. She would never come in with her socks all wrinkled down and her cardigan half off and hair all over the place. She would always look clean and scrubbed and neat and tidy. The teachers liked her as well. She was pretty and bright and fun and giggled a lot, but she was never vulgar or over the top about anything.'

Away from school Sophie was beginning to cultivate interests that would remain with her far longer than anything she learned from her textbooks. She had a family connection with the world of theatre and dancing and it was this great love of the performing arts that would later help to turn the head of a certain prince. Her early inspiration came from her uncle Thane Bettany and his wife Anne Kettle who were both members of the Royal Ballet. From the age of four little Sophie was taught ballet by Pearl Westlake, the elegant wife of the director of Sadler's Wells. These ballet classes at the beautiful Brenchley home of June Bowerman were the highlight of Sophie's week. Her regular partner at the classes was a local girl called Sarah Sienisi who became a long-standing friend and Sophie's first flat-mate when she moved to London. The only problem was that one of the girls had to lead. It was usually Sarah, and the girls were reduced to fits of giggles on numerous occasions. During the summer months June Bowerman would put on little shows in her back garden, which parents and villagers would come along to support. Sophie's mother was hugely proud of her daughter. When she appeared as Cinderella, with Sarah as the fairy godmother, Mrs Rhys-Jones could be seen wiping away her tears.

During one less serious performance Sarah and Sophie, dressed in hideous purple outfits, had to dance to Michael Jackson singing 'Rockin' Robin'. All went well until the record player began to slow down and, as the youthful high notes of the pop legend became a rich baritone, Sophie and her friend danced slower and slower while trying to keep a straight face. The audience roared their appreciation. One of the girls from those early classes did manage to find some fortune as a dancer, though not in the Royal Ballet. Philippa Williams became a member of the notorious dance troupe 'Hot Gossip', which, at the height of its popularity on the *Kenny Everett Television Show*, was regarded as highly controversial and 'naughty', although it would not worry granny too much these days.

The only part of those early performances that Sophie did not like was wearing all the stage make-up. She found it very cloying on her skin and this dislike of cosmetics has carried into adulthood — she always prefers to wear as little make-up as possible. Over the years Sophie managed to reach grade IV in dancing, which was quite respectable for a non-professional. The most memorable exam was when Sophie was nine and travelled to a school in Maidstone for her test. One of the other little girls suffered a bad attack of nerves and, as a result, left a puddle on the stage just where everyone had to run round in a circle. The whole thing became like a circus with all the little girls getting to the puddle and suddenly leaping in the air and jumping over it. Sophie found it hilarious. One of the perks of dance lessons was the regular trips to Sadlers Wells in London to see real ballet at first hand. Sophie loved it then as she loves it now, on the occasions when she and Edward slip off unnoticed to the Royal Ballet in Covent Garden.

Back at school, the nine-year-old Sophie moved up again to a building called Coursehorn, which was mixed, and to a more academic approach to schooling. Although Sophie was a bright and vivacious child she was not the 'Brain of Britain'. She's a good all-rounder and above average in most subjects, but her particular strengths lay in pursuits that demanded self-expression. That is why she loved ballet so much and also why she responded so well to her headmaster's fascination with drama. The Head was a middle-aged man called Robin Peverett who Sophie and her friends, with sparkling schoolgirl wit, called 'Mister Pervert'. They did not dare call him this to his face of course, as all the children were rather in awe of him. He was tall with dark curly hair and would usually wear a sober grey suit and dark glasses, which the children found somewhat menacing. He would stand in front of the school at assembly and no one would know who he was watching. He lived in a converted oast-house next to the school with his attractive Swedish wife Eva who all the children liked. He was keen on school discipline. When, for instance, two pupils complained about the food, they were made to stand on a table and eat their lunch standing in front of 250 children. Like all headmasters, however, he appeared far more forbidding to young children then he actually was. In reality, he was passionate about drama and would sport a bright red crew-neck jumper whenever he was in a theatrical mood. Although Sophie belonged to her village's dramatic group she was also much in demand to appear in some Greek tragedy or other that the Head was directing at school. Mr Peverett would make a special film of school plays which would be shown at the annual parents day. The important thing is that the headmaster liked Sophie and gave her the encouragement she needed to forge a lifelong interest in drama and the theatre. This would prove to be one more facet of her personality that Prince Edward found irresistible.

One of Sophie's favourite teachers was the English master James Bowler who urged her to write poetry and encouraged her fondness for Shelley and Keats and the Romantics, which are her chosen reading today. She was especially moved by Keats' *Ode to a Nightingale* — 'My heart aches and a drowsy numbness pains/My sense ...' — and learnt it off by heart, as well as composing many odes herself. The pupils would have to stand up in front of everyone and recite poetry, which required considerable nerve. She was not so keen on maths, although you would not have guessed so when she and her friends volunteered for the winter maths club, which was held on Saturday mornings. This was a typical schoolgirl gambit, because it meant none of them had to spend the time freezing to death on an outdoor activity. The maths teacher was called Jack Guy and to young Sophie and her friends he seemed very tall and quite terrifying. He did not have much hair, although he did have a moustache, and when he got angry the whole of his face would turn a bright purply-red. According to Janie Stewart he was a 'real Mr Chips'. After a while the girls began to regard him with a sort of grudging affection, especially because he cared so much about the school. He would treat the boys and girls in exactly the same way and would never address the pupils by their Christian names.

The school chaplain was a great character. The aptly named Trevor Vickery was known as Trev the Rev and he took Sophie's confirmation classes when she was 11. He was a very jolly fellow who rode around his parish of Staplehurst on a penny farthing. During the War Mr Vickery had been a physical training instructor on a cadet training ship, HMS *Conway*, which was anchored off Bangor in North Wales and it was there that he learnt the unlikely clerical pursuit of boxing. In those days he was, as he still is, a natural middleweight — 5ft 8in tall and 11st 2lb. Every Saturday morning while chaplain at Dulwich College Prep School, he held boxing lessons in the school gym and one term the girls, including Sophie, decided that what was good enough for the boys was good enough for them, too. So they insisted on lessons, which is how Trev the Rev taught Sophie Rhys-Jones how to box, for which she proved to have a modest flair. The girls were determined not to be seen to be the weaker sex. There was a great emphasis on sport at the school and Sophie impressed the boys with her running and swimming abilities. Her brother David was quite sporty, but Sophie could always hold her own when they kicked a ball around in the back garden. Sophie was no 'soppy girl' when it came to sport. Like many girls of this age, she had a tomboyish streak and enthusiastically joined her female pals in badgering Trev the Rev, who still remembers her as a 'lovely girl', to give them lessons. They all wore proper boxing gloves and learnt the rudiments of how to defend themselves. Prince Edward may have to take care if he should ever get on the wrong side of Sophie Rhys-Jones.

When Sophie was ten, she and her special friends Janie, Sophie D. and Tracy came across a book about witches called *The Ogre Downstairs*, which they passed round. That tale featured a wicked stepmother who put all the children through nasty witches' initiation ceremonies. This fuelled the fertile imaginations of the girls who decided to form their own school coven. Each week one of the four girls would be chief witch and would issue instructions or dares, such as being allowed only to wear certain colours or clothing. The most difficult, and the funniest, instruction came when Sophie decided they had to go all day without touching any metal. All went well until they trooped into lunch and had to try furtively to eat their soup without using a spoon. None of the teachers could work out why four young ladies were laughing so hysterically throughout the meal.

At Coursehorn there were about ten boys to every girl, which was quite favourable odds for the deadlier of the species. Unfortunately in the case of the four witches they all fancied the same callow youth, one Timothy Barker. This was the first time that the girls had shown a blossoming interest in 'nasty little boys'. Handsome Timothy was definitely the favourite boy in the class. He was a boarder and had a suntan from visiting his parents abroad. The girls were fiercely competitive about the object of their affections and would compose little notes or snatches of poetry for him and leave them in a desk where they knew he would be sitting, so that he would find them. The notes were quite innocent — suggesting, for instance, he should 'Meet me by the flowerbeds' or 'Meet me in the gym-hall'. The flowerbeds in question were outside the gym hall and were a collection of old pig troughs filled with brightly coloured flowers. It was by this set of romantic pig troughs that Sophie had her first chaste kiss with Timothy Barker, much to the chagrin of her schoolmates. There had been a fierce competition to see who would be the first to pucker up with Timothy, and Sophie won.

Timothy did not turn into a prince as a result of Sophie's kiss. It would be another 20 years before she kissed a real prince, but she had reached an age when her hormones were about to kick into a higher gear.

2

The Brenchley Belle

After passing her entrance exams Sophie moved on from Dulwich College Prep to Kent College for Girls at Pembury, a respectable girls' public school. As with many youngsters joining new schools she pretty much lost touch with the old gang. Not before, however, they had discovered the delights of raiding their fathers' drinks cupboards. Sophie and her friends would take it in turns to bring some alcoholic concoction to school. Janie Stewart remembers the hideous cocktails: 'It didn't matter what it was because you would pour it all together — a bit of whisky, some tonic water, a bit of gin, advocaat and all sorts of nasty things. We would put it all into one little tonic bottle and smuggle it into school. We used to hide behind a big sofa in the library and swig out of this bottle. We didn't get really pissed, but it was a dare. It was very exciting.'

Sophie had been a very robust little girl and was always fit and healthy. She was also one of the lucky ones who never had to wear an embarrassing brace and always had 'nice teeth' — a quality that has served her well over the past couple of years when the zoom lenses of the paparazzi have been getting more close-ups of her smile than her dentist. At Kent College her sporting prowess really came into its own and she was soon in the athletic, swimming, netball and hockey teams. She could run like the wind, but she excelled on the hockey pitch. Although she was not the tallest girl she had a reputation for being an animal with a stick and she struck fear into her opponents.

Her own sporting talents were dwarfed, however, by the exploits of the school celebrity — a girl called Suki Brownsden who became one of her best friends in those early teenage years. Suki was a fantastic swimmer and represented her country in the breast-stroke at the Olympics. She lived in Pembury with her parents who were close pals of Sophie's mum and dad and the two families socialised together. Sophie was a little in her shadow in those days because, as a swimming prodigy, young Suki was always zooming off to international competitions. Suki, who is now married, remains fond of her old friend and has seen her from time to time when Sophie's work for 'Baby Lifeline' took her to the charity's headquarters in Coventry, where the former swimming champion now lives. 'She is the same old Sophie and we still get on really well. We saw a lot of one another back then because our parents got on. I was very single-minded about my swimming and would spend a lot of time training or going to competitions. It wasn't a very big school and we were both very sporty. They say that your schooldays are the happiest, but I just wanted to leave and get on with my swimming.'

Sophie, too, was restless in her mid-teens. Pembury in Kent was quite isolated, even though it was just a commuter ride to London. Although The Bay City Rollers made a passing impression on Sophie and her friends in the mid-1970s — all their wardrobes contained a revolting pair of tartan trousers — they did not embrace the rapidly changing youth culture of the 1970s. The world of The Sex Pistols was a million miles away. The realisation that there was an inviting world away from Brenchley began to dawn on Sophie, especially as she became interested in boys. She had one big advantage over many of her schoolmates because she was a day-girl and lived locally, which meant that it was easier to meet the opposite sex. From being a young girl who was sociable but more of a follower than a leader, Sophie became much more boisterous.

She attended theatre workshops with her friend Sarah Sienesi at nearby Tonbridge Boys' School and it was there, while rehearsing an Arthur Miller play, that she met her first proper boyfriend. Sophie was 15 and not exactly shy. He was David Kinder, dark-haired and very handsome with a twinkle in his eye. He was also passionate about the theatre, a quality that Sophie finds irresistible in her men. David's parents lived in a splendid house in Chislehurst, near Bromley in Kent, and the teenagers would spend hours larking about on their tennis court. Sophie was on cloud nine that she had a real boyfriend at last — wrestling with a Bunsen burner in the school chemistry labs began to seem very juvenile to this young woman. She was embarking on the great love of her life, which, as is so often the case with 15-year-olds, lasted all of a couple of months before they got fed up. David went on to become a professional actor, but reached only the not-so-giddy heights of a part in *Doctor Who* and a McDonald's advertisement before deciding that the teaching profession offered more long-term security. He has remained on excellent terms with Sophie who he still describes as a 'lovely girl' and over the years she has often been a guest at his parents' home. One of the recurring themes in Sophie's life, which does her great credit, is her ability to remain on good terms with former boyfriends who, like David, all stress how lucky Prince Edward is. She must be doing something right.

Her growing interest in the opposite sex did not stop her from struggling through eight O-Levels, including art, history and French, which would prove invaluable when she embarked on a Swiss skiing adventure. Her strongest subject was English and Sophie has since confessed that, if she had the chance again, she would have liked to study literature at university. There was another factor to take into account when Sophie decided whether to stay on at school. The school fees for Kent College and Wellington School in Somerset, which her brother attended, continued to put a considerable financial strain on her parents. Her devoted mother persevered with her secretarial work to make sure the children had the best education. In the end Sophie decided to leave school at 16 and she enrolled in a two-year secretarial course at the West Kent College of Further Education in Tonbridge. Her reasons are familiar to thousands of girls — it was something to do and she would have a qualification at the end of it. Sophie made sure that she pursued her twin loves of English and the theatre. She started A-Level classes in English at the college and is very proud of the fact that a lecturer from the University of Kent at Canterbury sat in on one of those classes and told the teacher afterwards that, even at the age of 16, Sophie had the ability of a second-year university student.

Sophie went along with her pal Sarah Sienesi to an audition for the Cranbrook Operatic and Dramatic society, which, although local, was quite a prestigious group. Sophie thought the audition would involve her chasing around the stage as a member of the chorus. Instead, she had to sing a solo from *My Fair Lady*, which filled her with complete dread. Singing has never been one of Sophie's strong points, but she battled through with just a few dubious notes and landed a part in the chorus. The best thing about it was that, because she and Sarah had been taking ballet and dancing classes for more than ten years, they ended up teaching the dance routines to the rest of the chorus.

At secretarial college Sophie hit it off with another local girl called Jo Last, who became her best buddy for the two years that they were at college. Although Jo lived in the village of Goudhurst just down the road from Brenchley, the two girls did not know each other before they met on the first day of the new term. Jo had gone to Cranbrook State School while Sophie had been at Kent College. This was September 1981 when Soft Cell were at Number One with 'Tainted Love' and Adam and the Ants was the most popular teen band. The two girls would pass their days eating crisp sandwiches and moaning about boys. Jo remembers: 'We linked up on day one because we were in the same class and just hit it off. Sophie was so sweet and so funny. We would talk endlessly about things, mostly about what great things we were going to do with our lives and, of course, boys. Sophie would listen for hours while I would go on about my boyfriend who was called Simon. She was so unselfish about it. She had boyfriends, too, but no one especially serious at that time. Sophie was very pretty with great skin and the same sort of hairdo she has today. Best of all she always had a big smile.'

Every morning Jo would zoom down the winding

country road between Goudhurst and Brenchley to pick up Sophie from home. It took about ten minutes and she would toot the horn and wait for Sophie, who was always a punctual girl, to come out. Jo's father had given her the old brown Citroën as a present. She called the car Matilda and, although it was a bit battered and the sunroof stuck, the car represented freedom to the two friends. At lunchtimes they would hurry down to Matilda and zoom into Tonbridge to Bentalls' department store and gossip in the little café there. Then they would eat a packed lunch in Matilda before rushing back for afternoon classes. Their favourite lunch was salt and vinegar crisps packed into a bread roll with a Bounty bar for afters. Sophie has always been one of those lucky girls who has a healthy attitude to what she eats. If she wants a bar of chocolate she has never thought twice about having one.

These were very much carefree, fun-filled days, not least because the work was far from taxing. Sophie became an expert typist, due in part to her teacher's habit of bringing in tapes of Status Quo for them to bash away to, so that they would develop a good rhythm. The girls could type so fast to 'Rockin' All Over The World' that they re-named it 'Typin' All Over The World'. Sophie's growing spirit of adventure is best illustrated on the morning that the two friends set off to sit their English A-Level exam. Jo recalls: 'We were sitting in Matilda, doing some last-minute revision. Suddenly, at the same time, we both looked up, grinned at each other and threw all our notes out the window. We were still giggling uncontrollably when we entered the exam room. Everyone must have thought we were mad. Sophie passed with flying colours. I flunked it!' Besides English Sophie passed an O-Level in law and her exams in shorthand and typing, so she felt well equipped to find a secretarial job.

Away from college Sophie was enjoying a typical teenager's social whirl, although her adventurous streak meant that she was champing at the bit to move to London, which, while not very far away as the crow flies, was a hassle to get up to and back again without a car. The last train home arrived at Paddock Wood at 12.30am, just when things were getting going in the capital. Even then, there was the hassle and expense of getting a taxi home unless your parents were in a good mood.

So like many young people in the sticks, Sophie's social life revolved around the local pubs where she was the life and soul of the evening and very popular with the boys. In Brenchley itself there was The Rose and Crown or The Bull while just outside was The Peacock, which was popular because it was very noisy and, therefore, unlikely to attract any parents. One of the regulars at The Peacock, Stuart Cleary, remembers: 'Until they cleaned it up recently it was always the dodgy pub. We were all very friendly. We swapped lovers manically at that age and, to be honest, it's all a bit of a haze now. At the time I was living at Goudhurst in a place called Cherry Tree cottage and Sophie used to come back with everyone after a night out. Sophie wasn't permissive, but she was fun-loving. She was a bit pear-shaped and, therefore, very good at drinking. As far as I can remember she used to wear Puffa jackets and Hunter wellies.' Those wellies were much in evidence when everyone regularly piled off to the races at Charing and it was here that Sophie first got a taste for champagne, which always tastes delicious when served from the boot of a Range Rover.

On one memorable occasion, The Peacock set decided to hold a toga party in the sailing clubhouse on nearby Bewl Water. It was a riot. Everyone turned up wearing the skimpiest sheet they could find. The best chat-up line of the night was: 'Excuse me, do you mind if I just change the sheets?' The beer and the gin flowed throughout the evening and everyone became very merry. Unfortunately, that also included the guy who was giving Sophie a lift home in his Land Rover. On the way back to Brenchley he veered off the road, ploughed through a hedge and ended up upside down in a ditch. It could have been very nasty, but the gods were smiling and they were rescued by other friends on their way home.

The next thing Sophie's 'chauffeur', who would prefer not to be named, remembers is waking up on the floor of Sophie's living-room with her father standing over him offering him a cup of tea and a plate of toast. Sophie's dad was very popular with all her friends, always jolly and tolerant of the young folk. When she held her 21st birthday party at home he made a memorable speech thanking 'the Disco Johnny for providing the music'.

Her brother David had his 21st in the local Castle Hill pub when Sophie was just 17. Sophie was the life and soul of the late-night party, larking about in a black trilby, flirting outrageously with the male guests, downing gin and tonics and puffing away on her favourite Benson and Hedges cigarettes. Sophie smoked for many years although only socially and had given up by the time she met Prince Edward. One of the party guests recalls: 'Sophie was very extrovert that night. She did a high kick for the camera while she was hugging a friend. She was laughing and giggling and thought it was a hoot. She was never worried about getting a hair out of place and could hold her own in any drinking stakes.' Sophie was wearing her hair short and spiky and, dressed in a man's checked shirt and skin tight green jeans, her look might best be described as smart punk. David, with whom she has always got on famously, was decidedly the worse for wear by the end of the evening, which Sophie found highly amusing especially when he leaped over the bar and tried to pull his own pint. The ability to enjoy herself and just 'have fun' is one of Sophie's most attractive qualities and one that she has not lost.

*   *   *

Just outside Brenchley is a pub called The Halfway House where Sophie got her first job as a waitress to earn some extra pocket money. This pub is famous locally because it is reputed to be haunted by the ghost of an old woman wearing a long dress, a hat and carrying a handbag. A recent landlord, Dave Pollard, was very sceptical about this ghost, but he saw her one night standing absolutely still at the foot of his bed with a black dog at her side.

Another former landlord and his wife once put all the chairs in the pub's little restaurant on the table when they had finished for the night only to find next morning that they were all back on the floor grouped around one table, as if there had been a special gathering of ghosts and they had held a party. According to local legend the old lady can be a cantankerous ghost and is liable to break the place up every so often, like the time she ripped all the curtains down. According to local farmer Michael Noakes it is because the pub, which is about 470 years old, used to be a funeral parlour. He explains: 'The bodies were brought in and stored in the basement and then brought upstairs to a room behind the present bar for embalming. There is supposed to be a secret room with a staircase that has now been bricked in where you can hear strange creaky noises as if someone were climbing stairs.' Although Sophie knew all about the alleged ghosts the only spirits she saw were those being downed by the young men at the bar.

Coincidentally Princess Diana also started her working life as a waitress, in her case at a men-only gymnasium club in the City. It does not figure prominently on the Princess's CV and the fact that she was the most famous former waitress in the world remained a secret for more than ten years. She worked in the restaurant at Slim Jim's club soon after she came to London as a raw 18-year-old, before she became involved with Prince Charles and was, according to one of the club's staff 'charming and sweet'.

Back in secluded Kent, Sophie and her teenage pals discovered that there were plenty of good spots for romantic late-night trysts. One of the best was at Payne Farm where you drove up a dirt track, turned right at some apple orchards and parked for total privacy unless some other couple had thought of it first. Kite Lane, Short Lane and Flightshot Farm were also popular — although Sophie drew the line at Matfield Village Green, which was for exhibitionists only.

When she left West Kent College in June 1983 Sophie wasted little time in moving to London, equipped only with her secretarial qualifications and a sense of adventure. As so often happens she lost touch with Jo Last, although, in Sophie's defence, she made numerous attempts to try to trace her.

The problem was that Jo's parents moved away from Goudhurst. The two friends talked on the phone for a year or so after Sophie had moved to Kensington, but Jo went travelling in New Zealand and they drifted apart. Jo eventually met an American, fell in love and moved

6,000 miles away to live in Seattle, so it is hardly surprising that Sophie found it difficult to find her. After all this time Jo has nothing but kind words for her old friend: 'People have said to me, "Isn't she lucky to be marrying a handsome prince?" My reaction is that Edward's the lucky one for getting her. She is a normal, wonderfully down-to-earth decent girl. She'll be the best thing to happen to the Royal Family in years.'

3

A Capital Girl

Like any normal girl Sophie had quite a few boyfriends during her teenage years. When she was seventeen she dated a local boy called Robert Scott-Mackie, the elder brother of a schoolfriend. As any schoolgirl will tell you, elder brothers are always a good bet. She also went out with the village heart-throb, Andrew Miller, who was apparently 'the sort of guy girls always go for'. Sophie 'went' for him for a while. Footloose and fancy free she met a good-looking sporty chap called John Blackman and they dated briefly. Unlike the majority of teenage passions, her friendship with John survived their fling and he has remained one of her dearest friends and a generous and guiding influence. A few years after their romance, for instance, he organised a few friends to club together and buy Sophie her first skiing holiday for her 21st birthday. She immediately loved the thrill of whizzing down the slopes and has been an enthusiastic skier ever since — so much so, in fact, that it later proved to be one of the great turning points of her life. Up until the time she met Edward, Sophie would try to go skiing with John and his friends every year if she could afford it. He has always been her closest male chum and so it was a happy situation for Sophie, that when she took the plunge and moved to the capital, she was able to stay at his parents' house in South London while she looked for a job and somewhere more permanent to live. John was embarking on his career in computers and is now a partner in a highly successful computer software company.

Sophie, meanwhile, had put together her first CV and sent it to a host of prospective employers. She had taken advice at college and had decided that a job involving meeting people would be ideal. She was very sociable, confident and well-presented, so public relations seemed like a good starting point. She was lucky. Just a month after leaving West Kent College, Sophie landed her first job at the Quentin Bell PR Organisation in Covent Garden as secretary to the managing director, a promising start for someone fresh out of secretarial college. She stayed there for six months before moving to a similar sort of job with the Tim Arnold sales promotion agency. She was already beginning to carve a career path for herself, although at the time she was still just a secretary.

Although Sophie was firmly established in the 'Sloane' social life in Chelsea and Fulham, where she had found a flat to share with Sarah Sienesi, she still took every opportunity to pop home to Brenchley. For her 21st birthday party, Sophie wanted a black tie affair, so her father hired a marquee for the garden. It was such a windy afternoon and evening that everyone thought the marquee would blow over. The next day, those that could remember what had happened at the party all agreed that it was a great evening. One of Sophie's close friends, Michael Wilkins, was found by her father next morning asleep under a tree with his Walkman on his head and his dinner jacket neatly hung on a branch. Bodies were crashed out everywhere, but Mr Rhys-Jones took everything in his stride as he always has done where his daughter is concerned.

Another of her friends, Charlie Alson, could not find a blanket anywhere. After searching for what seemed ages he eventually stumbled across one and bedded down for the night in a tent in the garden. Next morning the family dog greeted him like a long-lost brother — it was the dog's blanket! At this time Sophie was going out with a chap called Rupert Keane who, conveniently, was her father's godson. Rupert is married now and lives in the 'Royal' county of Gloucestershire and, like the majority of Sophie's former flames, is still on friendly terms with her.

In 1986 Sophie struck gold when she responded to an advertisement in the media section of the *Guardian*. The job was press assistant to Jan Reid, the former *Daily Mail* journalist who was chief press officer at Capital Radio. At her interview Jan was impressed by Sophie, who in those days was a bit 'Sloaney' but not too much, and she gave her the job. In the early days her work was mundane — typing, administration, filing and responding to letters. Mike Whitehill, now a scriptwriter for Jasper Carrott, took over from Jan Reid and remembers Sophie well. 'None of us got any glamorous trips to begin with,' he recalls. 'We went to the opening of the M25. That's how glamorous it got. Some trip. But Capital was a fun place to work then.'

In 1986 Sophie's work changed and she split her time between the press office and the promotions department run by Anita Hamilton. It proved to be a turning point for Sophie. The two became great friends, even though Anita was her boss, and are close to this day, meeting regularly for a drink and a gossip. Anita was a firm believer in everyone working and mucking in together, so Sophie's job was never clearly defined.

There were four people in her department — Sophie, Anita, Rhona Martin (who is now with the Prince's Trust) and Karen Levesconte (who works for the England Rugby team) — and they were very much a gang. Most days after work the girls would 'go over The Square', which was the local Capital Radio pub and socialise with other staff. Sophie loved working at the radio station, which was a very happy workplace but also gave her the chance to broaden her skills. She had the opportunity to meet heroes like Mick Jagger who chatted with her when he came into the station. Her day-to-day work included helping to organise launches and photocalls and writing press releases, usually about what the DJs were doing. It was clear that Sophie was adept at the most important part of PR work, being nice to people while chatting over a glass of wine. The DJs, or Disco Johnnies as her father would have called them, were always in the public eye and getting on with them was major part of Sophie's job. In that respect, she was very popular.

TV presenter Michael Parkinson's son Andrew became a special friend while he was producing the David Jensen show at Capital. Sophie found Andrew, who was very popular in a Mr Rugby Club sort of way, extremely good company. He had a store of great stories about the celebrities whom his father knew.

When he was a youngster, George Best came to stay with his family and Andrew and his two brothers took on the great man in a game of football. They had to get the ball off Bestie, but he was not allowed to let the ball touch the ground. George won. To rub salt in the wound, he had to listen to George making love to Miss World, Mary Stavin, all night long in the next bedroom. Although Andrew and Sophie dated only about four times over a period of six weeks he has some startling insight into her ambitions: 'She used to have friends at Capital, but frankly she was more interested in friends who had titles. She was always going on about places she'd been to and parties in the country. That's the kind of lifestyle she always wanted. I think that beneath a very bubbly and sometimes busy character, there lurks somebody who knows their own mind and where they're going. We went out a few times and had a bit of fun. She was never serious. I would describe her as happy-go-lucky.'

Sophie's eye for social cachet is confirmed by Mike Whitehill who says: 'She always used to, I recall, come back from weekends a bit hungover, a bit worse for wear, because she had been away for the weekend with a Giles or a Jeremy. She likes people of interesting status, the aristocracy and stuff. She was always impressed by titles. You would often hear her talking about these people. They sounded like complete tossers, but they obviously impressed her. She was blinded by that sort of thing. She had a very full social life. I remember there was one boyfriend she was stuck on for about a year. She was besotted by this chap who I think worked in the City. She would often come in , as girls of that age do, and be silent and morose. It would eventually emerge that it was something he had done. The next day it would be all sunshine and roses.

I remember that being a bit of a pain in the arse, to be honest with you.'

Neil Fox started at the station in September 1987 and, as Doctor Fox, is now the second-biggest star there after Chris Tarrant. He remembers that all the DJs saw a lot of Sophie and he is very complimentary about her: 'I bumped into her all the time. As a new boy I was always out doing gigs and roadshows and she would help organise everything for me. She was always smart, not a jeans and T-shirt person. Anita Hamilton was always smart as well and I think Sophie followed that line. She wore nice skirts, blouses, scarves and trouser suits, that sort of thing. Capital was an exceedingly friendly place in which to work. Anita, Sophie, Rhona and Karen were a nice little team and they are still good friends. She was just one of the girls, a good laugh and a good company person. She was not particularly flirty, but I would describe her as having a good, lively past. She was a nice Sloaney kind of girl. There was nothing about her I didn't like. She was very good-looking and the kind of girl who could go out with a group of lads and have a really good night, drinking beer and telling dirty jokes like anyone else. She was a fun girl, not a druggie or a bonker, just a normal girl.'

Like many young, free and single girls who are 'lively', Sophie has always had to suffer the gossip-mongers. One of the stories doing the rounds was that four men, who all worked for the same media company and in the same office, discovered in the pub one night that they had all been out for a drink with Sophie at one time or another without any of the others realising. They are then supposed to have stood up at the table and toasted her in champagne. It's the sort of story young women have to put up with. You have a drink with someone and everyone immediately thinks you must be having an affair. Andrew Parkinson describes her lifestyle as 'colourful'. He observes: 'I think Sophie lived life to the full. Her big weakness, if anything, is that she enjoys herself and it could be interpreted incorrectly.'

The most famous 'affair' Sophie is supposed to have had is with Chris Tarrant, who is a radio superstar. The truth of the matter is that the two of them hit it off right away. Tarrant is brilliantly funny and makes Sophie laugh. Although he is now happily married, he has, in the past, enjoyed a reputation as a Casanova, a reputation that has been fuelled over the years by stories in the tabloids. The principal source of all the rumours about Tarrant and Sophie comes from a photograph taken by Chris Tarrant's former co-presenter Kara Noble, now a DJ with Heart FM, while they were doing the show in Spain. Someone from the publicity department would always go on the trip to look after clients and any competition winners who were there as well. In this particular photograph Sophie is sunbathing topless on a beach and looking very gorgeous. She is fast asleep and totally unaware that Chris Tarrant is hovering over her glistening body like a cat eyeing a huge tub of clotted cream. The photograph, which Andrew Parkinson says is the 'stuff of myths and legends', took pride of place on the noticeboard of the DJ's room at Capital HQ for years, until it was revealed that Sophie was going out with Prince Edward. Then the picture disappeared faster than a ferret up a trouser leg. No one knows what happened to it, but someone has the negative. Doctor Fox, who has seen it hundreds of times, observed: 'It's just one of those innocent pictures, but if someone wanted to make something out of it ... I am sure there was nothing in it. I would say Sophie is a "pro" who wouldn't get her honey where she gets her money.'

Sophie and Chris have remained excellent friends and Sophie also gets on particularly well with his Norwegian wife Ingrid, another bubbly blonde. For his part, Tarrant never indulges in tittle-tattle about anyone and for a man who makes more than a £1 million a year from opening his mouth everyday he is almost perversely quiet about his private life. The only time you get a peep out of him is when he is plugging a show, like the love-it or hate-it *Man O Man*, where ten defenceless blokes compete in front of 300 noisy women for the dubious privilege of being the only one left standing after a series of elimination rounds. Chris then treated *Sun* readers to such titbits of information as not being able to remember the name of the girl he lost his virginity to at 19 on a secluded riverbank.

Foreign trips were certainly one of the perks of Sophie's job with Capital Radio. By far the most memorable was when she joined Doctor Fox and other pals on a ski club trip to the resort of Courmayeur in the Italian Alps, which was considerably enlivened by the presence of Marino Franchi, the stripper and porn star who is known in the business as 'Superdick', and is a familiar sight on Cable TV's Fantasy Channel. Italian-born Marino, who sports flowing dark locks and an easy Latin charm, proved very popular on the trip, especially with one of Sophie's girlfriends from Capital who took a particular shine to the man who was dubbed a 'professional penis' by *Cosmopolitan* magazine and who claims he can maintain an erection for eight hours. Marino went on two ski trips, but Sophie was only on the second one. A couple of his friends had heard the first trip advertised on Capital and persuaded him to join them there at the resort of

Madesimo . This was before Marino had made it big in the sex world and was earning a living with a knife-sharpening business. He became good mates with the people from Capital, including Sophie's boss Anita Hamilton, and was delighted when Rhona Martin from Capital phoned up and invited him to join them the following year. 'She's an absolute darling,' purrs Marino, who has slept with over 1,000 women.

Marino took a shine to Sophie because he remembers she was 'a lot of fun' although he does admit that his mind was on other things for most of the holiday. He smiles, 'I was involved with a certain woman from Capital who was quite high up' — as she would be if she were with sexpert Marino. Sophie needed all her sense of fun when Marino played a prank on her one evening. 'I was having a fling with this stunning friend of Sophie's and she put me up to it. We decided to break into one of the Capital girls' hotel rooms. We chose Sophie's room because she seemed to be one of the best sports. We broke into the room and rifled through the undies she had already worn. We chose a couple of pairs — they were white with a pattern on them — and wore them to the disco that night.'

It was a typical holiday disco with loads to drink, bad music and happy laughter. All the time that Sophie was having fun with her friends she had no idea that Superdick was wearing a pair of her best Marks and Spencer's knickers on the most famous part of his body. 'We were at a table in a sort of booth at this club so there was plenty of privacy. All the girls were there and I started to do a slow striptease. They were all laughing and shouting and cavorting at the sight of me stripping off until I just had Sophie's undies on. Then Sophie looked at me and said "God, you've got girls' knickers on. What a giggle!" Then I could see the realisation dawn on her face as all the other girls laughed and she twigged. "They're my knickers. They're knickers I've already worn!" Then Sophie herself started laughing and she shouted "You filthy pig!" Everybody was still laughing and she jumped up and screamed and charged back to the hotel.'

Since those reckless days — that was the last of the Capital ski club trips — Marino's career has gone from strength to strength. His talents are not confined to his lunchbox because he is also a singer and dancer, a demon on a motorbike and an accomplished fire-eater. He is also the star of *The Lovers' Guide*, probably the best-known of the explicit sex education videos with lots of BCUs (known in the trade as Big Close Ups) of Marino showing the viewer how to pursue delights such as intercourse and oral sex. Now he earns more than £2,000 a week, drives a top-of-the-range Mercedes and is doing a job he really enjoys. 'I get through an average of six girls a week but if there's a rush on, it could be more.' Although Marino would never presume to give Prince Edward advice, one useful tip that male strippers often employ is to tie a piece of elastic around the base of their penis to trap the blood, which enables them to maintain a good line and length throughout their act. The slight drawback is that Superdick is likely to become Purpledick by the end of the performance. Although Marino has kept in touch with Rhona Martin and one or two others from Capital, he has not spoken to any of them since it was announced that Sophie was going out with Prince Edward. 'Are you kidding? They wouldn't touch me with a barge-pole,' he says with disarming honesty.

On another trip, this time to Florida, Sophie played matchmaker for one of the top DJs at Capital, Graham

Dene, who presented the Breakfast Show before Chris Tarrant and now works for Virgin FM. Sophie and Graham, who says she was 'lovely to work with' were among the Capital gang looking after a party of 75 listeners on a charity trip to Disney World. They had all paid £475 for the weekend jaunt, which was in aid of Help A London Child. When they arrived at the hotel — the Sheraton — everyone was sorted out with a room and piled into the lifts. Graham recalls: 'I got into the lift to go up to my room with a lot of other people. My room was on the first floor, but someone pressed the button for the top floor and so we had to go up there. When everyone got out there was just me in one corner of the lift and this beautiful girl in the other. All I could think of saying was "Oh hello". It was the start.'

The girl in question turned out to be Julie Tennant, a gifted artist and, by coincidence, related to the great English artist Turner. Julie had gone on the trip to cheer herself up because she was down in the dumps due to boyfriend trouble. She certainly was not looking for romance, but she caught Graham's eye. The next day when everyone was racing around Disneyland he made a point of seeking her out. Sophie, who had noticed how well they were getting on, insisted that they put their arms around each other for a photograph, the very first of Graham and Julie together and one of their most treasured mementoes. Although they were getting on well nothing happened on that weekend — not least because Julie's boyfriend inconveniently turned up — but Graham took her phone number and the photograph back to London and resolved to call her at the earliest opportunity. Their first date was to a Prince's Trust concert at the Royal Albert Hall where Graham introduced her to

Princess Diana at the reception afterwards. Diana is on record as saying that Graham is her favourite DJ and she hit it off instantly with Julie. Four years later in 1992 Graham and Julie returned to the Sheraton in Fort Lauderdale, shared the same lift to their room and got married.

Back in London Sophie started her first serious relationship with an 'older man'. Jeremy Barkley, who she called Jez, was 11 years her senior and sold Sophie her first car, a Morris Minor, which does not sound like the start of a relationship calculated to send a mother's spirits soaring. Jeremy, who was one of identical twins whom Sophie could never tell apart, was her boyfriend for nearly two years, which was her longest single relationship until Prince Edward came on the scene. Sophie has described Jeremy as a 'Jack of all trades', but he is a successful businessman who runs a Reading-based company that sells air-conditioning.

Although Jeremy was older than Sophie, he never curbed her natural spirit of adventure and they never settled into being an 'old married couple'. Towards the end of their on-off relationship, when it was becoming more off than on, Sophie began to get itchy feet. Some of her friends at Capital were moving to new jobs and, even though she enjoyed the work, she felt in a rut and wanted a new challenge. Sophie was 24 years old with a world to explore and she started browsing through the ads for a new start. Her relationship with Jeremy officially ended on amicable terms. He remains a bachelor and says of his former love, 'I will always have a place in my heart for her.' Sophie's mind was made up when a friend suggested doing a season's skiing working for a holiday firm. She loved skiing so set about applying for jobs. One of the tour companies, Bladon Lines, took her on and so she decided to leave her old life at Capital Radio and see what lay in store for her on the ski slopes. That future turned out to include an exciting romance.

4

Ski Fundays

Before she could set off for the snow in a glamorous ski resort Sophie had to prepare for her new job in the not-so-rarefied atmosphere of Putney, a couple of tube stops away from the Sloane playground of Parsons Green. She joined 50 prospective reps at the offices of Bladon Lines on a series of training days that would equip her for dealing with all the problems that could leap out at you when you are responsible for someone else's holiday. Sophie had to learn the company's policy for dealing with such difficulties. The new season's reps had to attend the week's course even if they were experienced and had done the job before. From Bladon's point of view, throwing 50 people together and seeing how they coped gave the company the chance to see if the young men and women were suitable for the job. Gareth Crump joined Sophie on that training course in late November 1990 and he recalls: 'The most important thing is confidence and the company wanted to make sure you had enough of it to deal with all types of situations. I remember that Sophie was a pretty girl wearing her hair longer than she does now. She was very easy-going and friendly. She wasn't one of those dizzy sorts.' Sophie has never been short of confidence and passed the training 'audition' with flying colours. She found that most of the others were like her, in their mid-twenties and a bit fed up with how their life was shaping up — Gareth Crump was training to be a lawyer — and looking for a change even if it was only for a few months to collect their thoughts and decide what they wanted to do next. Everyone had to speak a foreign language. Sophie was fluent in French, although she did take a few night classes to brush up.

Sophie was posted to Crans-Montana in the Swiss Alps. Her contract ran from the beginning of December to mid-April, a period known in the holiday trade as the 'season'. She was issued with her blue Bladon Lines uniform, which made her look a bit like an air hostess, said her goodbyes and set off on her four-month-long posting little realising that it would turn out to be a much greater adventure than she had ever imagined. The only slight regret she felt as she flew out of Heathrow was that she would not be home for Christmas. That has always been a special time for Sophie and her family and this would be the first Christmas she would not celebrate in Brenchley.

To reach Crans-Montana you have to fly into Geneva and then get a coach or a train through 200 kilometres of the most inspiring scenery. Everyone, no matter how many times they have flown to Geneva, catches their breath at the first sight of the magnificent Mont Blanc. The ski parties usually travel by coach to the resorts. Most of the holiday disasters tended to happen in the

French resorts where you could spend ten hours on a coach travelling to and from Geneva. Crans-Montana was less than three hours from Geneva and quite isolated. Sophie was soon to realise how lucky she was to have been posted there. Crans-Montana was originally two adjoining villages in the heart of the Alps that had grown into one over the years. The twin resort is spread over the sunniest of all Alpine plateaux dotted with lakes and larches and Sophie was awed by the scenery sweeping from the forbidding slopes of the Matterhorn to the shimmering splendour of Mont Blanc. Crans is the more upmarket part with fashionable and expensive boutiques selling Gucci, Louis Vuitton and Chanel and the more exclusive restaurants and discotheques. This part of town boasts one of the largest Alpine shopping centres where the majority of the shops would leave a credit card burning a very large hole in your pocket, so they were well out of Sophie's price range.

As a ski rep she made the princely sum of £50 per week. There was, however, no need to send for Red Cross parcels because her skiing equipment, passes, food and board were all taken care of, leaving the £50 as pocket money for things like drinks, shampoo and Swiss chocolate, which Sophie loved. When she was there, the money went a lot further than it does today because there were nearly three Swiss francs to the pound. The Montana end of town was the hub of the action and the late-night bars and clubs proved a magnet for the reps, chalet girls and ski instructors. It is a long-held tradition that during the day all the girls ski into their ski instructors and at night it is vice-versa. This was true in the lively days of the 1960s, but now many of the ski instructors are over 50 and family men. Sophie, however, was fortunate enough to hitch up with a young Australian ski instructor.

Before she could think of affairs of the heart Sophie had to settle in to her new life. Christmas was approaching, but there was no time to be homesick. She was in charge of Chalet Isabella, a large three-storey chalet in the Montana district, which could sleep 42 people. There were kitchens on all levels and bunk beds for the young chalet girls who cooked and cleaned. They were the most important people in the resort because the entire operation could be reduced to chaos without them. They are also the last group that you want to upset. One former chalet girl in Crans-Montana, who for obvious reasons wants to remain anonymous, explained: 'If somebody gave us a hard time or was unbearably rude we would clean the toilet with their toothbrush.' Sophie, who had her own room at Chalet Isabella, proved very popular with the chalet girls, who were really just versions of her old Sloane self. She was responsible for five girls and had to keep an eagle eye on their work. She also had to get her head around the chalet accounts and sort out any insurance problems if, for example, one of the guests broke a leg. Some evenings she had to think up things for the clients to do — the *après-ski* programme, as it was called. The most difficult times were when the chalet girls had the evening off. Sophie soon hit upon the idea that a fondue evening would be fun on these occasions because it would get everyone talking and mucking in together. They proved to be a great success, although the downside was having to deal with a group of chalet girls all nursing sore heads the next morning.

By far the most important thing in the life of a resort and therefore of a rep is the skiing itself. Sophie had been in love with the excitement of whizzing down the slopes ever since she went on her first ski holiday at the age of 21. She quickly discovered she was going to have plenty of time to ski in the afternoons after she had finished her morning work and before the holiday guests came back in the evening. Sophie, who had always taken her sport very seriously, decided to take a refresher course. This proved to be a good move. Her instructor was a young Australian called Michael O'Neill, six feet tall, athletic and dark with the brooding looks of Madonna's ex-husband Sean Penn.

There was an instant spark between the two young people. Sophie had never met a man like Michael before. He was quiet and considerate but at the same time had a devil-may-care attitude that was light years away from the precious media types and the Fulham 'hoorays' with whom she had spent so much time over the past few years. He was a breath of fresh air. He spoke of sailing in Sydney Harbour and surfing on Queensland's Gold Coast and she was swept along on a romantic wave that never reached the shore. Sophie's friends back home in London might well have been astonished at how quickly she settled into a daily routine with Michael. To all intents and purposes Sophie spent the season as Mrs O'Neill. In the evening they would meet other instructors or reps at some of the bars like Bar One, Bar Two, Valentino and Absolut where Sophie could let her hair down and dance to Michael Jackson and Phil Collins. It was blissful.

One of Sophie's closest friends in Crans-Montana was Valerie Lafone who supplied the crockery and cutlery to the chalets. She noticed the tell-tale signs that Sophie was in love during their regular get-togethers. Three or four times a week they would meet at a little pâtisserie just around the corner from Bar One in Montana. 'I noticed a big difference in Sophie after she met Michael,' remembers Valerie. 'Suddenly she seemed to enjoy her work more, although it was very demanding. She became generally more radiant.' There was one final piece of evidence that convinced Valerie that Sophie was in love. She recalls: 'I noticed she was losing weight.' Sophie told Valerie that she and Michael would go on trips away from Crans-Montana, driving to the neighbouring exclusive resort of Zermatt or skiing off-piste under the shadow of the Matterhorn.

As part of her routine Sophie would travel to Geneva airport once a week. All the resort reps would gather to return their holidaymakers to the airport and greet their new parties. They would sit around drinking coffee and catching up with the news while waiting for the incoming flights, although Sophie, displaying a quality she has never lost, was very discreet about her own romantic arrangements. Gareth Crump, who was posted to the fashionable resort of Meribel, recalls: 'Usually we would talk about the skiing we had been doing or if there had been any disasters the previous week like the plumbing breaking down. Sophie was always pleasant and calm. She could be quiet at times, but just because she was happy to be that way not because she was shy. And she certainly wasn't flirtatious.' What the other reps did not know was that this was because Sophie had eyes only for Michael O'Neill.

Not everyone thought as highly of Michael as Sophie. A Dutch woman called Christina van Heerden who worked at popular nightclub Dacha, says: 'He complained a lot. He was not always complimentary about this area and he was sulky. He was here for a few years and was even interviewed by a TV crew. The girls liked him a lot.' It was not easy for Sophie and Michael to spend time alone together because privacy was at a premium in Chalet Isabella or at the ski instructors' lodge. To check into a hotel would cost anything between 50 Swiss francs (£17) to a year's wages for a four-star hotel. The couple discovered that the only thing they could afford was a tent for £4 a night, which was about as attractive as skinny-dipping in an Eskimo's fishing-hole.

Christmas is not celebrated to great excess in Switzerland and most families enjoy a quiet dinner, exchange of gifts and a church service. Sophie, however, was determined to have a splendid Christmas dinner, just like home with roast turkey and all the trimmings. She helped the chalet girls to prepare a lavish meal for the holiday guests and invited Michael, for whom Christmas surrounded by snow-covered peaks was quite a contrast to spending it on the beach back home in Australia.

The season flew by in a flurry of skiing, skating and snowboarding — something that Sophie found she was particularly good at. She also found that her skiing technique improved in leaps and bounds. Sophie remained her sociable self and popular among the local shop and bar owners. One of them, Christian Rey, supplied Sophie with her skis and boots: 'I particularly remember Sophie of all the reps. She was very pretty, but the great thing about her was that she would pop in for a chat. She didn't have to. She just made the day brighter by doing so.'

As April approached Sophie and Michael turned their thoughts to the future. At her weekly coffee breaks at Geneva Airport the other reps were all cavalier about doing another season the following year. Sophie was uncertain. Michael was returning to Sydney, a place he made so inviting with his descriptions of the barbecues, climate, surfing and easy-going lifestyle. It was a long way from home, but Sophie had always wanted to see the Sydney Opera House and the Harbour Bridge.

Sipping her cappuccino, she examined her alternatives. She could return to London with no job lined up and nowhere to live and try to find work for the summer, thousands of miles away from Michael. Or, perhaps, just maybe, she could take matters into her own hands and fly to Sydney with him. 'What's wrong with being crazy?' she thought, as she greeted the last batch of holidaymakers. They could always come back to Europe together to do another season. Who knows what adventures lay in store in Australia. Sophie took very little persuading when Michael hesitatingly suggested that she should go back with him to Oz. She jumped at it. It all sounded so tempting. And Michael would be there. Just like Shirley Valentine, Sophie decided to let the dream continue. She would become 'Sheila' Valentine.

5

Sophie Down Under

Sophie's dream of a wonderful life with Michael did not last long. All too quickly it dawned on her that the love affair was no more than an extended holiday romance. They were both a long way from home in the snows of the Swiss Alps and love came easily. In Sydney Michael was on his home patch, secure and comfortable and eager to show off his lovely new girlfriend from England. Sophie was thousands of miles from friends and family, excited at the challenge of adapting to a new life and culture and not ready for anything 'comfortable'. Inevitably they realised they wanted different things and split up. Although Sophie was bitterly upset that things did not work out, she was determined not to crawl home to Brenchley to lick her wounds. She was and is made of sterner stuff. The fact that she has never mentioned Michael in public is a strong indication of how the split affected her. She has always freely admitted to past boyfriends like Jeremy

Barkley, John Blackman and David Kinder, but that list has never included her handsome ski instructor. Michael still lives and works in Sydney, but has kept his head down where Sophie is concerned. A friend observed that if Sophie's name was mentioned, it was clear that Michael still thought fondly of her and that, although he has never mentioned it, he is probably still in touch with his former love. The friend added, 'He never mentions why they split up and is extremely loyal to her.'

A knight in shining armour arrived in the shape of Andy Cullity, who she had first met at parties around Fulham and Chelsea in the early 1980s. Sophie moved into the house that Andy shared with friends in the fashionable Paddington area of Sydney and he convinced her to give Australia a real go for a year and make the most of it. Andy, who is six years older than Sophie, then 24, worked for a courier company, TNT Skypac, and he introduced her to Jonathan Miller, a local businessman and the boss of another international shipping company, Jet Services. Jonathan was immediately impressed by Sophie's dynamic attitude and gave her a job as his Girl Friday. It was manna from heaven for Sophie. She was responsible for preparing invoices, booking in couriers at the airport and chasing packages half way around the world. 'Her main work was answering the phone and typing,' explains Jonathan. 'The great thing was that she didn't mind what she did — including making the coffee.' Thanks to her secretarial training Sophie had no problems with the work, which, while certainly not as glamorous as her previous job at Capital Radio, gave her the freedom to enjoy fabulous Sydney and make many friends with whom she still keeps in touch. Andy agrees that Sophie fitted in well: 'She has a personality that people here can relate to. She's a get-up-and-go girl who doesn't sit back in a prim and proper English manner. The great thing about Sophie is that she is a very strong person and doesn't let things get to her. Basically, she was just a young English girl travelling around Australia for a year.'

At night Sydney comes alive and, unlike the London that Sophie had left behind, it never closed. You could drink in the clubs around King's Cross until dawn. The Paddington area close to the university was a trendy mix of bars, including gay cabaret joints, which, while not exactly family entertainment, were places to go and have a good time. And Sophie was having a very good time. She bought a battered VW Beetle and zoomed about the city. Australian men loved her sense of fun and the fact that she would swig anything from a bottle — not bad for a Pommie bird. 'She was so bright, bubbly and vivacious,' remembers Jonathan Millar. 'We used to socialise a lot after work and she always had loads of friends.' For her part Sophie quickly realised that the most objectionable Australian men are usually the ones who have found their way to Britain. She did not turn into a wild party animal, however, spending many evenings looking after Freddie Miller, her boss Jonathan and his wife Karen's baby son.

At weekends Sophie would join Andy and his girlfriend on trips around New South Wales and up into the Blue Mountains above Sydney. Many of the tourists to Australia forget there is such a beautiful landscape around the country's largest city and leave having seen nothing more than the Opera House and the Harbour. That was not Sophie's way, although she loved sailing around the Harbour and also joined a deep-sea diving club, which became a great passion. Almost everyone she met at barbecues or parties invited her to go sailing. It was on one such idyllic trip around the secluded bays of the south-east coast that she met a dashing graphic designer. Eon Balmain was in his mid-thirties, dark and tanned like many of the men in Sophie's life up until Edward. Eon, an unusually romantic Australian, says: 'I took one look into those beautiful blue eyes and thought "Wow!"'

Eon and Sophie were among a group of ten young amateur sailors spending two long lazy weekends on a luxury yacht called the *Meridien*, which, while not exactly the Royal Yacht Britannia, seemed like a floating palace to Sophie. There were crystal chandeliers in the state rooms, twelve beautifully furnished cabins and even a spa, or hot-tub as Americans call them. Their host was a millionaire retired naval officer and businessman, John Young, from Cairns in sunny Queensland, who had personally invited Sophie on the 'voyage'. He moored the 100-foot schooner, his pride and joy, in Broken Bay, north of Sydney. While the boys and girls shared the chores, John was the master chef preparing meals and supervising the nightly barbecue on deck. Eon Balmain, who had changed his name from the less exotic Ian Robinson, had been invited on the trip because he had done the artwork for John's yachting caps and T-shirts. He and Sophie hit it off immediately because they had both worked in radio and had lots of anecdotes to swap in the sun. He recalls Sophie fondly: 'She was just captivating. She is very, very attractive, so vivacious and beautiful. When she walked on board wearing a pair of tight-fitting shorts the whole wharf drew breath. Most of the time she wore a flimsy sarong, which really turned me on because she looked so sexy in it. She has a great little figure and she had a light golden tan to go with it. She looked wonderful with her fair hair, streaked blonder in the sun. I think she was the most attractive girl I have ever met.'

This was a sojourn not far short of paradise for Sophie and her shipmates. The days were spent sunbathing on deck with a good book for company, jumping off the boat for a swim in the bathwater-warm sea or sliding, firmly clutching a glass of champagne, into the hot-tub where their host John would pour his own concoction of soothing bath oils — the perfect way to end a busy day doing nothing. A net had been strung across the stern and everyone took it in turns to splash about in it, held safe by the momentum of the vessel. Sophie loved this and would giggle and splash around like a happy dolphin. Sophie was also the best at a game they all played called 'walking the line' where you had to tiptoe as fast as possible along a line painted on the deck.

One evening after everyone had enjoyed more than their fair share of drinks, danced energetically to 'La Bamba' and relaxed in the hot tub, Eon, emboldened by the sea air, slipped into Sophie's cabin. He remembers: 'I've got to confess that my intentions were not strictly honourable. I was hoping for more than a goodnight hug. Sophie was alone in bed, half asleep with a sweet smile on her face and the sheets pulled up under her chin. We'd had a great day on the booze and I honestly thought my luck was in. She was looking so gorgeous, but my luck wasn't in. It's hard to believe but all I did was tell her the story of *Sleeping Beauty* as if she was a child about to go to sleep. When I had finished the part where Beauty is awakened by her prince's kiss I saw that Sophie was sleeping like a baby, so all I could do was sigh and tiptoe out, shutting the door behind me.' It was to be a few years before Sophie would kiss a prince for real, but she could certainly dream about it. Coincidentally Prince Edward slipped into the conversation when Eon told Sophie how much he admired the Royal Family, little realising that she would be joining them. He told her he had been to London and seen the Trooping the Colour ceremony and how great he thought it was. Sophie was delighted that Eon was not in tune with the anti-Royalist feeling that has swept Australia in the past few years. As a portent of the way she would embrace Prince Edward's life in the future, she impressed Eon by refusing to join the band who were forever knocking the Royal Family.

Eon recalls that Sophie was very discreet about her past. She retained an air of mystery and never joined in discussions about lovers past or present. The ability to be discreet is one quality with which Sophie appears to have been born and it was later to become an important reason why she was so welcomed into the Royal Family by the Queen. Eon had hoped to see Sophie again to pursue their friendship. 'She was very easy to talk to, with a very quiet and sympathetic side as well her natural vivacious personality. I told her that my mother had died of cancer and she responded like she had known her personally. She seemed very upset. I told her how wonderful she was and she said she would see me on a cruise later in the year. But she never showed.'

These jaunts in and around Sydney convinced Sophie that she should see all of Australia if she possibly could. Encouraged by Andy and Jonathan, she saved her pennies and, after being in Sydney for nine months, decided it was time to move on. There was no longer a special man in her life, so she joined up with a Scottish girl called Lynne Muir who she had met in Sydney and who was also travelling around the southern continent. She and Lynne travelled north to Queensland, visiting the picturesque Whitsunday Islands and diving around the magnificent Great Barrier Reef and on to Cairns, a tropical city in the middle of

Australia where Sophie performed the ultimate game-for-anything stunt and went bungee jumping, a thrill she loved. She did not know it at the time, but she was incredibly lucky to have had all these wonderful experiences before she met the Queen's youngest son. It would be rather unseemly for a princess to be seen bungee jumping off Tower Bridge. If Sophie were a man, everyone would be saying how fortunate she was to have sown her wild oats in her twenties and be ready to settle down in her thirties. Diana, for example, never had that chance and it does not take a psychology degree to theorise that the Princess of Wales was far too young and naïve when she got married.

In June 1991 Sophie decided to come home. She had been away a year and she missed her family. Most of all she wanted to make it back in time for her Dad's 60th birthday. There was going to be a big party with another marquee set up in the garden at Brenchley. She knew her mother and father wanted her to be there and she was not going to let them down. She also wanted to see her friends and tell them about her adventures. She travelled back via Thailand, so that she could stop off for ten days on the paradise island of Koh Samui. She arrived back home on one of the wettest and windiest June days imaginable. It reminded her of her own happy 21st when everyone had thought the marquee would blow away across the lawn. Over drinks and the subsequent lunch party all the guests asked her endless questions about her travels Down Under. As the heavens opened and it cascaded with rain, she thought of those sun-kissed days of sailing and sunbathing. It was good to be home.

6

Starting Over

Sophie had no job, nowhere to live and no boyfriend. She was 26 years old when she returned from Australia at a time of year when everyone else was excited by their summer holiday plans. She was luckier than some in that her parents were always delighted to see her and reassured her that she could spend as long as she liked at home. Most of her friends were in London, so Sophie decided to try to find work there. The first task of the returning traveller was to prepare a CV, which was a good deal more impressive than when she had left London 18 months earlier. Now she had travelled, had worked for an international company and had undertaken much more responsibility. Encouraged by her mother and father, she decided to move into the world of promotions and public relations.

Her CV found its way to the Cancer Relief Macmillan Fund in Chelsea, which hired her to work with the National Promotions Manager Jill Phillips organising special events. A former colleague recalls: 'She was so full of energy. It inspired everyone to do their best.' In effect it was just an extension of her work at Capital Radio, but Sophie found it particularly rewarding. That was just as well because it was not very financially rewarding, a starting salary of just £12,000 was barely enough to pay the rent. It is also an essential interest for any budding member of the Royal Family, where helping to raise money for good causes is the principal occupation. Even though she now has much more prestige through her Royal connection Sophie continues to work for the Macmillan Fund on a private basis, serving on one of the committees. She explained: 'The Macmillan nurses do the most incredible work and I shall always have a special affection for them.'

Now to find somewhere to live. Here Sophie struck lucky close to home. She was introduced to an air hostess called Ulrike von Herwath whose parents had a lovely house in the neighbouring village of Benenden. Her stepfather is Charles Lennox-Connyngham, a relation of the Spencer family and the former boss of Sealink. Ulli's family were minor German aristocracy, but her main claim to fame was that at her public school in Huyton, Lancashire, the big joke was that she could not fit all her names on her O-Level exam forms. Ulli is tall, blonde and striking and she was a superb diver as a girl and easily won all her school competitions. Her swallow dive was particularly impressive. An admirer of Ulli's enthuses: 'She is absolutely drop-dead gorgeous — she is to die for.' Ulli and Sophie immediately became firm friends and Sophie moved into the spare room at her attic flat in Vereker Road, West Kensington. The houses there are three-storey and painted white with heavy black doors. The road is a commuter short cut and always busy with traffic. It was, however, a perfect location for a single girl like Sophie whose social life revolved around Chelsea, Fulham and Kensington. It was also handy for her great friend John Blackman who lived in Earl's Court.

They say things always happen in threes, so all Sophie needed now was a boyfriend. She soon found a solid respectable one called Tim King, who has a dental practice just over Albert Bridge. Tim also had a glamorous, exciting hobby that Sophie found thrilling. He was a keen pilot and every weekend they would be up in the skies, often flying across the Channel to Le Touquet for a night out. Their relationship was almost brought to a shuddering halt the first time he took her for a spin when the plane's engine failed and he had to make an emergency landing, which left them both shaken but fortunately uninjured. Sophie has never been a girl to let a spot of danger put her off and she could not wait to have another go. Tim even flew her down to Andorra for a weekend's skiing. The break got off to an unlucky start when Tim had to make yet another emergency landing because of bad weather, but this time he put down at Bordeaux Airport, which was slightly embarrassing, as their predicament brought the entire airport to a standstill. After a while the romance with Tim started to cool, but it had been fun and they remain very good friends. Tim is still her dentist, although Sophie has always had beautiful teeth so he never has much to do other than telling her to 'have a rinse'.

Sophie has never been one to let the grass grow under her feet and, single once more, she was happy to be carefree. One of the most memorable weekends was a three-day party thrown by Ulli at her parents' home in Benenden. The invitation sounded like a menu for a

Roman orgy. It tempted guests with the promise of 'cosmic croquet, visual vibes, mellow munchies, dizzy juggling, BBQ, dancing, tennis and swimming'. Ulli introduced Sophie to an old friend, a German student who had driven over for the party. In these pre-Edward days Sophie had a much more casual appearance, a hangover from her time in Australia. Her hair was longer and blonder and she was happy in T-shirts and jeans. She really was fancy-free and free to fancy her German admirer. They played tennis and drank and swam in the open-air pool and, as he later ungallantly revealed to the *Sun*, shared the same sleeping-bag. It was a memorable weekend, but on Monday it was back to work.

When her contract at the Macmillan Appeal ended, Sophie was ready to dust off her CV yet again. This time, however, an old friend from Capital Radio recommended her to Brian MacLaurin, a go-ahead Scottish PR executive whose small agency was rapidly expanding and who had many contacts in the media from his time working as a television producer. Brian has great energy and drive and a sharp sense of humour, qualities he could see at once in Sophie. He recalls: 'The minute I met her I knew she was an absolutely charming person.' Sophie joined the company when it had been up and running for about a year and had offices in Victoria, but after six weeks they moved to new premises in Hammersmith, which was handy for Sophie's home. At the time she was one of a staff of seven, but within two years she would be part of a team of 18. Sophie was an account manager and in the early days with MCM (MacLaurin Communications and Media) was chiefly office-bound. Brian, however, does not hide his staff away. He observed: 'Sophie grew into the job. There is no hierarchical structure here. We are all part of a team. We don't have any promotion or anything like that. You simply earn more money as the company becomes more successful.'

At this stage of her career Sophie did not have great business contacts and relied on Brian's judgement to steer her into accounts where she could be of most help. One of his clients was Chris Tarrant, Sophie's great mate from Capital Radio days, and she was able to work well with him. She also did marketing work for the children's favourite Thomas The Tank Engine. Sophie enjoyed promoting some of the female characters in the stories. She explained: 'When I was a child *Thomas The Tank Engine* stories were pretty much a boy's thing. But now I am a big fan and if I was young now they are something I would have some affection for. The Refreshment Lady character is very much a 1990s figure — she's a businesswoman.' Sophie herself was on the way to becoming very much a 1990s woman, successful and independent. It could be said that being the Queen's son's girlfriend for more than three-and-a-half years without marrying him is the ultimate gesture for a modern young woman.

Her biggest triumph at work came when she was helping with an account for Mobil Oil and she managed to get Gene Pitney to agree to let his great hit 'Twenty Fours Hours From Tulsa' be used in a commercial for the petrol station. She was so chuffed when his manager told her it was agreed that she squealed down the phone: 'Tell him I love him and I will have his babies.' The singer heard about this and was so amused that he mentioned Sophie frequently on his concert tour in 1993 and repeated her offer. It is a lovely story that demonstrates Sophie's natural and almost innocent enthusiasm, which is something she shares with Prince Edward. Sophie also enjoyed helping Brian once a week on the *Noel Edmonds' Garden Party* show, although it is not strictly true to say, as newspapers do, that she did the PR for Mr Blobby.

Of more significance to Sophie was the Baby Lifeline account. This charity, whose profile has been raised considerably through its association with Sophie, was founded fifteen years ago by Judy Ledger, a vigorous Coventry housewife who had tragically lost three premature babies. She decided to do something to help other young mothers who might suffer the same fate and since then has been raising money to buy equipment for hospitals to try to save babies born prematurely. Since she started the charity as a small local help group it has expanded into a national concern and raised £2.5 million to buy equipment and aid research into neo-natology. Judy may glean some satisfaction from knowing that babies born now, even more prematurely than her own, have a fair chance of survival. Sophie became involved when another MCM client, Heart FM radio, recommended her. Judy has nothing but praise for Sophie, with whom she felt an instant rapport. She points out: 'Sophie could create a story out of a paper bag and I immediately liked the ideas she put forward. Sophie is very determined and is so genuine in her interest in the charity.'

One of the most welcome changes in Sophie's life at this time was that she had jumped several salary grades and was now making more than £20,000 with bonuses. She did not have to rely on a rich boyfriend to pay for everything. She could also go away at weekends and pay her own way. One of her favourite weekend jaunts was to Devon with her friend John Blackman's cricket team. She would drive down with friends to the village of Stoke Fleming on the coast south of Dartmouth and get away from it all. First stop on Friday night would be the local Green Dragon pub where the drinks and the laughter flowed in equal measure. On Saturday the agenda would include a little swimming and a great deal of sleepy sunbathing. Sunday afternoon was match day. John's team was known as the Fentshire Cricket Club, a made-up name for a group of ambitious friends who worked hard in London all week and wanted to play hard at weekends. Sophie joined old girlfriends like Alison Crane and Gwen and Sian Lloyd Edwards who she had met in the early 1980s when she had first joined John Blackman at Stoke Fleming. It was around this time that he had decided to reorganise the village cricket team and hit upon the idea of getting his London friends to join him. Sophie is not really interested in cricket but dutifully helped to make the ritual tea. She would also do her bit by preparing the massive team suppers, which were the social highlight of the weekend. Sophie is a very loyal friend and as a result her friends are very loyal to her. These weekends were as cosy and comfortable as a favourite pair of slippers. Even after meeting Edward, Sophie has made sure that she has time for her friends.

In the summer of 1993 life was good for Sophie. She had a busy social life, many friends, money in her purse and a challenging and enjoyable job. Just one thing was missing ... a prince.

Part Two

7

Light Entertainment

When Prince Edward was 24 years old, he was approached by the journalist Alice de Smith, then a 15-year-old drama student, in his capacity as patron of the Cambridge Youth Theatre. She asked him directly: 'Given the chance and if you weren't a Prince of the Realm, would you become an actor?' He replied without hesitation: 'Yes, I would.'

*　　　*　　　*

As girls tend to do, Sophie grew up considerably faster than Prince Edward. Many observers believe that Edward has started to mature only since he met Sophie. She has given him stability, and the means to escape the stranglehold of pomposity and arrogance that are part and parcel of the privilege of his birth. One of the more fascinating questions about their love affair is which one will have the greater effect on the other. It is like a battle of two Draculas. Will Sophie become full of airs and graces or will Edward relax, become more fun and more like the 'ordinary bloke' he professes to be? The signs so far indicate that we can look forward to the latter scenario, although Sophie would be a Wonder Woman if she remained entirely the same.

She is bound to change. Edward is barely recognisable as the same angelic-looking young prince who braved the Spartan world of Gordonstoun school near Elgin in Morayshire. It is well documented that his elder brother Charles looks back on his schooldays as the most miserable of his life, loathing the school with a passion. It was less austere by the time Edward took the high road from Balmoral, some ten years later in the autumn of 1977.

Edward confirmed this, saying, 'I don't think Gordonstoun is as tough as it used to be,' although the morning ritual remained the same. Everyone had to drag themselves out the back door, run eighty yards down the drive to a large tree and then back again, but not to bed. A hot shower was followed by a bracing cold one to shake the final semblance of sleep from youthful bones and ready them for the coming day. Edward's entire life seemed to be one great bun fight in those days. There was very little privacy, so he learnt to exercise a great deal of self-restraint. He was in a house called Duffus (not Duffers!) on the western edge of the school's estate, where conditions were a little cramped to say the least. The Prince slept with 25 other boys in a dormitory that could have fitted into the nursery sitting-room at Buckingham Palace. Beds were squeezed in head to toe and Edward just had to grin and bear it.

Edward candidly told his biographer Ingrid Seward: 'I don't agree with the statement that schooldays are the happiest days of your life. A school is a school and it is only one chapter in my life.' He did, however, indulge and develop many of the interests that he has taken with him into adult life — sharing these pursuits with Sophie Rhys-Jones has been one of the reasons why their relationship has flourished where others have floundered. The two principal areas that inspired him were sport and, to an even greater extent, the theatre. His housemaster James Thomas recalls: 'The thing that interested Edward above all else was drama.' His drama teacher, John Lofthouse, confirmed: 'Edward lived for acting.' He quickly became a driving force in school drama from the moment he took the lead in a Duffus house production of Peter Schaffer's *Black Comedy*. He also played Paris ('a man of wax and a flower') in *Romeo and Juliet*, the main school play one year. Before they were married Prince Charles took Diana to see Edward's own production of a Feydeau farce called *Hotel Paradiso*, which had been a 1960s film starring Alec Guinness and the gloriously voluptuous Gina Lollobrigida. The production became more farcical than the play itself because it took place in the open air during a downpour. All the young actors slipped and slid around the stage to uproarious applause from the audience, who laughed in all the wrong places.

The teenage Edward had a well-meaning, yet distinctly juvenile sense of fun, which he did not grow out of until after the *It's A Royal Knock-Out* débâcle when national respect for his family was sadly undermined. When, for instance, he appeared in *Hay Fever*, the Queen and Prince Philip came up from Balmoral, a three-hour journey by chauffeur-driven limousine. They had reserved seats and Edward hit upon the jolly jape of sticking labels on the backs. Instead of 'Her Majesty The Queen' and 'Prince Philip', they read 'Mum' and 'Dad'. To his credit, Edward never minded what job he did when he was involved in the theatre, which was just as well when, much later, he had to make the tea at Andrew Lloyd Webber's Really Useful Company. One of his contemporaries at Gordonstoun was the actor Jason Connery, son of Sean, who once had the distinction of directing Edward in a school performance. His view of the young Royal actor was 'he listens hard and he learns fast.'

Edward's theatrical obsession spilled over to the holidays when he would organise entertainment for his close family. He would generally write and star in these one-man shows. One of his early efforts was about a man in a potting-shed. Edward, of course, was not to know that his future love would do some starring of her own in a potting-shed before they met. His was a monologue. Hers was a double act in a sleeping-bag with a handsome German lawyer, who would sell his story to the *Sun*. It is quite ironic that Edward's love of the theatre was nurtured as a child by his love of make-believe. For any other child that fantasy world would have reached its zenith in pretending to be a Royal prince. Ingrid Seward suggests that Edward learnt to mix with people from different backgrounds at Gordonstoun. That is perhaps true only in that anyone Edward mixed with was going to have a different background from the Queen's youngest son. Gordonstoun is a privileged society where the boys and girls are all from middle- to upper-class backgrounds.

Edward could hardly fail to be reminded of his position when he was always addressed as Prince Edward by the master or Your Royal Highness by any visiting bigwigs. Intriguingly, James Thomas remembers that the lower down the social strata you were, the more familiar you were allowed to be with the Prince. His close school-friends called him Ed. Not surprisingly this very formal state of affairs did little to discourage Edward's pompous streak. When he was in the sixth form, for instance, he went over his housemaster's head and wrote directly to the laundry complaining that his shirts were not folded well enough. It did not go down too well. It also flies in the face of Gordonstoun's legendary toughness to know that pupils had their shirts laundered for them.

Like Charles and his father Prince Philip before him, Edward rose to become headboy, a position called Guardian at Gordonstoun. He was also head of his house. Yet even before he had that authority Edward was quite straight-laced, especially where school rules were concerned. On one occasion he stumbled upon a group of boys enjoying a smoke and some vodka in the grounds. Instead of joining them Edward shouted: 'Get back to your house captains. I'm reporting you for this.' Punishment for smoking and drinking would have been the threat of expulsion, although it is an interesting comment on changing social attitudes that these days the offender is instructed to take a long walk and contemplate the error of their ways. Edward was very similar to Sophie at school — neither were the goody-two-shoes they seemed to be, but both were adept at disappearing before the punishment police arrived.

The most obvious difference between the Gordonstoun of Prince Charles' experience and that of Prince Edward's was the presence of girls. The school went co-educational in 1972, so Charles just missed out.

The founder of Gordonstoun, a German-born Jew called Kurt Hahn, did not regard sex as a suitable subject for a schoolboy and, as in many public schools, it became a covert activity. Transgressions were frowned upon and shortly after Charles left one sixth former was banished after being caught in bed with two maids.

Girls were a great civilising influence on the school and Edward, although likely to blush in their presence, was considered a charming young man by the female population, if a trifle prone to taking himself too seriously. Another considerable advantage of having girls about was that they could take the female roles in school plays, thereby sparing the boys the embarrassment of having to parade in dresses in front of their peers.

Away from school in those days Edward did not have to suffer the intrusion of scoop-hungry paparazzi or journalists chronicling his every move. He was able to go unnoticed to cinemas in the West End for the latest James Bond film, to bookshops to buy his favourite thrillers or to record stores in search of Abba (a band he was potty about). It is unthinkable that the Edward of today could pop into Our Price and check out the latest Peter Gabriel CD (his current favourite artist). It is sad to see how recent events have chipped away at the Royal Family's trust. Edward, perhaps as much as any, is compulsive in his pursuit of privacy, something with which Sophie has had to come to terms.

Edward and his cousin Lady Sarah Armstrong-Jones would sneak out to the shops of Chelsea and Knightsbridge. In those teenage days Edward really fancied himself as a disc jockey and at Windsor he would assemble his Royal contemporaries, including Sarah, her brother Viscount Linley, Lady Helen Windsor and Marina Ogilvy, in 'Eddie's nightclub', which doubled as a drawing-room during the day. After dinner Edward would put Abba or Boney M on the turntable and the youngsters would indulge in some awkward disco-dancing. If Edward had ever been a professional disc jockey it would have been on Radio Two or the Light Programme, as it was previously called. Then Sophie could have phoned up with a request for a Dire Straits record.

One quality of the Royal Family that has been obscured is that the Queen's children get on very well together and they also have a good relationship with their parents. As the youngest, cherub-faced Edward was indulged but he also had the opportunity to be included in all their pursuits. Much later Sophie was pleasantly surprised at how close Edward's family was. Perhaps because he is the youngest, Edward has always shared a deep bond with his mother. He has inherited her strong desire for privacy where the family is concerned. It is hard to believe but as long ago as the 1960s the Queen created an enormous fuss when the *Daily Express* published a picture of her in bed holding Edward in her arms shortly after his birth. No one is better than the Queen at keeping emotions under control and remaining Royal at all times, but Edward strives hard to follow her example. The only problem is that when he lets his guard down it tends to be at the worst possible time — as at the press conference for *It's A Royal Knock-Out*.

More surprisingly, perhaps, Edward is his father's favourite son. Although he might appear delicate, Edward has never been weedy and at the tender age of seven would tag along with Prince Philip and learn how to shoot rabbits. He became an accomplished marksman and father and son would go duck shooting on the Sandringham estate, which involved them spending hours crawling through reeds. Shooting remains an important part of the Royal Family's social agenda and one that Edward has embraced enthusiastically. Sophie has discovered that one of the surest ways to a prince's heart is to act as a beater, disturbing the birds with sticks so that the men can blast them out of the skies. Beating has traditionally been the role of the lower classes while the shooting is strictly for toffs. No wonder Sophie was eager to learn how to shoot. Edward's father also taught him to sail and Edward still loves Cowes Week every July.

His sister Anne, who called him by the pet name of Nig Nog, turned him into a decent horseman and kept a pony for him at her home Gatcombe Park. She also has a strong sense of 'Royalness', which would have rubbed off on her younger brother. On one memorable occasion in Australia a photographer shouted for her attention, 'Look this way, love'. Anne froze him with a glance and barked, 'I'm not your love, I am Your Royal Highness.' It is no surprise that, as she has matured into middle age, Princess Anne has become more and more like a second Queen. Although he may not appear to have too much in common with his brothers, it was Charles who first trod the boards that Edward grew to love so much. The Prince of Wales, sixteen years older, was also an enthusiastic actor at Gordonstoun and always encouraged his younger brother.

Academically Charles and Edward followed a similar path to Cambridge. Considering that he had been given the unwelcome title of Educated Eddie by the press, Edward's A-Levels were far from special. He managed nine O-Levels which was a record for his family. He scraped three A-Levels with undistinguished grades — a 'C'-grade in English and two 'D's in History and Politics and Economics. These grades won him a place at Cambridge, which, although it was not really Edward's fault, generated a great deal of controversy. In any case those grades would probably be worth an 'A' and two 'B's today. They were more than enough for a young man planning a career in the Royal Marines. Edward had been a gentle boy and he was to become a

gentle man, happy to drift downstream on a course that had been well prepared in advance. He was not and has never pretended to be a playboy prince or a young girl's catch of the day.

On his eighteenth birthday he was pictured with his black Labrador Francis on, of all things, the cover of *Dog World*. It was a sweet photograph and as a result Francis received many fan letters. He also featured alongside Prince Albert of Monaco as one of the teenage 'Princes of Europe' in an American magazine for girls. The readers were advised that they could write to Edward at Buckingham Palace and they did — in sackfuls. His former private secretary Adam Wise recalls: 'We had to carry the letters off in tea-chests.' Edward was always very unassuming about his appearance, happy to sport unfashionable cords and tweed jackets despite the urgings of his female cousins to wear 'groovy flares' (at least he got that right). He did, however, develop an obsession about having his shoes polished so that he could literally see his face in them. He would even do his own. His other little vanity was keeping a comb in his top pocket so that he could constantly comb his already-thinning hair.

Despite his many good qualities Edward has never lost the knack of quite startling arrogance and petulance. A classic case was during his pre-university stint as a teacher in New Zealand. It has become a tradition that the Royal sons would have a spell in the colonies after they left school. It was good PR and gave them the chance to sow a few wild oats away from the spotlight. Charles had gone to Australia and Andrew to Canada, so Edward was left with New Zealand. He was found a position as a junior master teaching English and some PE at Collegiate School in the town of Wanganui. One morning he picked up the telephone to discover that on the line was Bryan Rostron, a reporter on the *Daily Mirror* in London and a confirmed Republican. Bryan, who was equally surprised to have got straight through to the Prince, politely introduced himself. Edward blew his top and shouted: 'Just what the hell do you think you're doing? You've got a nerve. What on earth gives you the right to call me?' Bryan, dogged in his pursuit of a story, replied that he had merely wondered how Edward was getting along as a schoolmaster. 'Well, your curiosity has just killed you,' blasted the hot-headed prince. Bryan, now sensing a decent scoop, asked, 'Killed me?' 'Er, in a metaphorical sense', said Edward, perhaps sensing he had overstepped the mark. He went on, 'This time I won't do what I could do to you.' Bryan asked what that might be. 'I will do something. Something rude will happen to you. [Long pause] Do you know what you have just done?', asked Edward, trying to muster a sinister tone. 'No,' replied Bryan. 'Well,' said Edward 'you've just done it!' The funniest thing about this conversation, recalls Bryan Rostron, is that Edward did not hang up. 'He was being very petulant, but he was too good-mannered just to say goodbye and hang up, which would have been the sensible thing to do. I wasn't going to finish the conversation, so I kept him on the line for half an hour and eventually we talked about James Bond.'

At least *Daily Mirror* journalists were nowhere to be seen on his trip to the South Pole, which he later described as 'probably the most memorable week of my life'. He followed in the snow prints of Scott and Shackleton and stood on the exact spot where he could see north in every direction. He visited the base camp from where Scott began his tragic last walk and visited Dry Valley, the driest place on earth with an annual rainfall of just 5mm of water, which either evaporates or is blown away leaving it free of ice and snow. He also joined the Antarctic Ski Club, so exclusive it makes Gstaad and St Anton seem like slopes for the hoi polloi.

The 'people' were generally not too happy that Edward had waltzed into Cambridge with such flimsy A-Level results. In advance of his arrival at Jesus College, a debating group called the University Republican Society was formed. The student newspaper *Stop Press* (and *Varsity*) carried reports speculating that students who might be hostile to the Prince were being vetted. The paper also suggested that students who had signed a petition against Prince Edward's admission were subjected to discreet security. Some students believed that the college authorities made photocopies of the petition, so that they could keep an eye on potential troublemakers.

Much of the storm had dissipated by the time Edward actually arrived in the autumn. *Stop Press* used his arrival to argue for the abolition of the Cambridge independent entrance examination, so that apparent abuses of the system could be avoided in the future. That is now the case. One student explained: 'At the time Edward applied Cambridge had their own entry examination, which was called 7th-term entry. You could also get a place through exams and an interview or through your A-Level grades, which are the main criteria now. Many students thought Edward got in through a telephone call from the Queen. It would be an aberration if he got in with the grades he had. If you could get in just because you are a Royal it would seriously devalue any degree from Cambridge. You must remember that there were hundreds of students with better grades than Edward who had applied at the same time to the same college, but didn't get in. The feeling was he was taking a place that somebody else should have had.'

In the end Cambridge went very well for Edward. He enjoyed a certain level of freedom, which allowed him to grow up far more than he had been able to in the insular world of Gordonstoun. Putting aside all the bleatings about his grades for a minute, it could be argued as being right and proper that members of the Royal Family should go to Oxford and Cambridge and mix with the best brains of their generations. It is at institutions such as these that the nation's religious and moral values are forged for the next twenty or thirty years. Edward fitted in well, particularly with the students. He took the first steps towards his ideal of being treated as an ordinary bloke by being plain Edward Windsor on the student list. He would go out of his way not to use his title. If he was not exactly Joe Bloggs, he was at least Prince Joe Bloggs. A former student observed: 'From the very moment he came up he wanted to show he had the common touch.'

Edward was very sociable and was invited to practically every party. The word would go round that he was going to attend and many students would turn up to see whether he would get tiddly and get off with someone. Edward would never dream of doing such a thing in public. Edward did a three year-degree course in two parts with archaeology and anthropology as part one and history as part two. During the second part he studied the history of the Royal Family and would have good-natured rows about some of the facts with the academics. Edward had his own anecdotes about his family and would counter and challenge where he did not agree with his tutor's appraisal. He was slightly disappointed when he achieved only a 2:2 grade in his degree because he wanted to do better than Charles who also achieved a 2:2.

Much more important than the degree grade was the lifestyle, which gave Edward the time to cultivate his interests, particularly in drama. He would go to lectures in the morning if he felt like it and a couple of times a week he would have a supervision, which is the term for tutorials at Cambridge. He had to write one essay a week and submit it the night before his supervision, so that he could discuss it with his tutor the next day. Edward became a familiar sight around town, riding his bicycle to lectures with his bodyguard pedalling furiously to keep up with his charge.

Cambridge has a deserved reputation for being the best university to go to if you want to be an actor, an actress or just a star. A long list includes Emma Thompson, Hugh Laurie, John Cleese and Stephen Fry — and Prince Edward who became the life and soul of the The Cambridge University Light Entertainment Society (CULES). Edward realised this was probably his last chance to indulge his passion for acting and he intended to live it to the full. The chances of him being allowed to audition for a BBC mini-series after obtaining a degree were somewhere between slim and non-existent. A performance by Edward was considered a great event and an ordinary college play would be 'sold out' every night if he was in it. Ironically, at the time he was a much bigger draw than some Kenneth Branagh-type. His poor detective would get heartily sick of having to watch the same performance night after night.

Although he made his début during his first term, playing the judge in Arthur Miller's *The Crucible*, Edward in the main eschewed serious drama in favour of the light entertainment society, which put on their shows at hospitals, old people's homes and even pubs.

As he had been at school, Edward was game to try anything, including song and dance, impersonating a drunk and pretending to be a yokel. Like Sophie, Edward is a talented mimic and does a sketch of Mike Yarwood impersonating Prince Charles that gives the original a good run for its money. Cambridge was the Yellow Brick Road for Edward because he could give full rein to his banana-skin sense of fun without fear of ridicule. In the real world this would not always be the case, as he later found out with *It's A Royal Knock-Out*. His many stunts included driving a taxi through the streets with two fellow students dancing on the roof and being tied to a railway line in the path of an oncoming train in the manner of a silent film heroine.

In his second year at university Edward contracted glandular fever, news of which spread like an epidemic through campus. 'Edward has got a snogging disease', was the whisper. As anyone who has ever had this complaint will know, the only thing you can do is take things easily for a while. For Edward that meant no rugby and no frenetic theatrical performances. Although it was an unwelcome inconvenience, the illness proved a watershed for Edward and in some ways helped to forge his future career. From performing he turned to producing and put together a children's entertainment called *The Tale of Toothache City*. Edward was involved with every stage, as he now is at his own production company Ardent. He told his biographer Ingrid Seward: 'I actually began to find that I really enjoyed putting things together and trying to turn what was an idea into a reality.'

As Edward was to discover, the role of producer/ impresario is akin to walking through a minefield — you never know when something unexpected is going to blow up in your face. On one occasion he was

entertainments officer for a May Ball. It was an early taste of the nightmares that can befall an impresario. The celebrity bill featured magician Paul Daniels — who was subsequently represented by the agency where Sophie worked — 1970s favourites Mud and the inimitable Gary Glitter and The Glitter Band. At 8.00pm Edward had to deal with local residents phoning up to complain about the noise, which was a little worrying as the fun did not start until 10.00pm. Edward and the others on the organising committee had agreed in advance to keep the noise levels down to an acceptable level. The only problem was that was not the acceptable level for Gary Glitter who proceeded to blast out 'I'm the Leader of the Gang I am' at full volume. When one of Edward's committee went to ask them kindly to keep the noise down, he was curtly invited to 'F-off'.

8

Girls, Girls, Girls

Considering that he has never enjoyed a reputation as a Romeo, Edward has not done badly and has cut a dash through several eligible young ladies. He has never had to endure a 'Randy Andy' tabloid handle like his brother Andrew. That is quite fortunate as it would probably have been 'Beddy Eddie'. The rumours about his sexuality that refuse to go away have cast an unjust shadow of incredulity over his relationships with women. The truth is it is just not that easy to find a suitable girl when you are the monarch's son. As Peter Townend, the veteran social consultant to *Tatler* once observed: 'Prince Edward has always preferred girls with interesting careers. The Queen would have preferred him to marry someone titled, but Edward has never been interested in the deb scene. His circle is theatrical.' Just how ridiculous life can become in the rarefied atmosphere of Royalty was clearly demonstrated when Edward set sail on what was christened the 'Royal Love Boat' in September 1992. He was one of ten princes and half a dozen princesses who gathered for a grand house party thrown by the King and Queen of Norway. The idea was to shuffle all the unmarried and eligible royals under 30 and hope that you end up with a pair or two. The actual occasion was the celebration of King Harald and Queen Sonja's silver wedding anniversary. In reality it was an opportunity for Cupid to draw back his bow. As is usual where Edward is concerned, Cupid shot himself in the foot. All the ingredients were there for romance, particularly a cruise around the fjords in the Norwegian equivalent of the Royal Yacht Britannia. Edward was linked (the tabloids' favourite word when there is absolutely no evidence of romance) to Princess Martha Louise of Norway and to a nobleman's daughter, Astrid De Schooten Whettnall. To surmise that Edward would be engineered into a romance is not to know the man. He is fiercely independent and it is no coincidence that he would meet his great love — Sophie — purely by chance.

Edward is supposed to have lost his virginity to a servant girl, a scenario that seems straight out of a made-for-television film starring Jane Seymour. The story features in Ingrid Seward's biography of the Prince, which was written with his co-operation. Apparently after he left Gordonstoun at the age of 18 he was seduced by a maid, a mature 21-year-old. One warm August night at 'Immoral Balmoral' she crept into his small first-floor bedroom and had her wicked way with the innocent prince, who was unsure if he was still dreaming. It was a hard lesson for young Edward. Before he could wipe the smile off his face, the story was all around the castle. According to one of the footmen, she walked into the staff dining-room the next morning and announced as 'bold as brass' that she had taken Edward's virginity. Here was a first and painful example of a situation that has recurred time and time again. His other biographer Paul James explained: 'Too often Edward has discovered that girls are only interested in him because of his status.' The Firm and Edward in particular will not tolerate a blab. It is why there is grudging respect for Royal consorts like Koo Stark and Camilla Parker-Bowles, both of whom would apparently go to the guillotine before revealing the bedroom secrets of Andrew and Charles.

Edward had stumbled across his first real girlfriend while he was still a shy sixth-former at Gordonstoun. Her name was Shelley Whitborn, a vigorous outdoors type of girl who, in the summer of 1980, nursed Edward's much loved pony Flash back to health while working as a trainee groom for Princess Anne and Mark Phillips at Gatcombe Park. Edward was extremely grateful and when he returned to school started writing to her with his news. Shelley, with her charming lack of airs and graces that so pervade young debs and Sloanes, was perfect for Edward as he stepped uncertainly into the sexual zone. He is cautious about relationships. In many ways this early friendship with Shelley, someone completely outside the Royal circle, has helped pave the way for Sophie. Both their fathers, for example, were involved in the motor trade — Shelley's father sold spare car parts in the Guildford area.

Edward made the leap from pen pal to boyfriend three days before the wedding of elder brother Charles to Diana in late July 1981. Princess Anne and Mark Phillips held a celebratory party at Gatcombe to which all the estate workers were invited. It was a warm summer evening and there was beer and wine, laughter and dancing in front of the house. Edward bided his time, sipping a dry sherry to summon up the courage to ask Shelley, who was wearing her best frock, to dance. It was a big step for a shy prince with what appeared to be the whole world watching him, ready to snigger if he got into a muddle. He waited until the soppy sounds of John Lennon's 'Woman' filled the night air and then marched over to Shelley and asked her to dance. Poor Shelley was teased rotten next day by the other grooms who mockingly called her Viscountess Whitborn. It did not matter because it had been such a happy evening.

Their first real date ended in disaster. Shortly after the fairytale wedding of Charles and Diana, Edward invited Shelley to come to London and see the new James Bond film *For Your Eyes Only* on the big screen in Leicester Square. Mark Phillips kindly agreed to lend Shelley one of the estate's cars, a Ford Fiesta, so that she could drive up to London. It was a very innocent evening. They saw the film together unnoticed and afterwards Edward waved her off on the road home. So far so good, no one would ever know about their evening out. At least that would have been the case had Shelley not ploughed into the back of a trailer carrying a rare and newly restored Alvis Speed Twenty coupé on the M4 near Theale. The unfortunate Shelley had lost concentration, perhaps dreaming of her own Royal wedding. Luckily she was only slightly hurt when she banged her head on the steering wheel, suffering only a slight concussion.

She was, unsurprisingly, very shocked and confused when the police arrived at the scene to inspect the wreckage. When she told them where she had been and where she was going, the officers' reaction was along the lines of, 'A likely story miss. Pull the other one.' A police spokesman confirmed: 'She was talking about a party she had been to with Prince Edward and saying she was on her way back to Gatcombe Park. The officers were suspicious, but later discovered she was telling the truth when they contacted the car's owner.' Hurrah for Captain Phillips! Having concluded that Shelley was not a joyrider, she was taken to the Royal Berkshire Hospital in Reading from where her parents rescued her. The night to remember had turned into a night she would never forget. A subsequent £80 fine for careless driving would serve as a permanent reminder.

Edward was the perfect gentleman about the whole affair. Instead of dumping Shelley he asked her to Buckingham Palace, this time insisting she caught the train and stayed the night. The scenario was ripe for seduction. After a light supper in his rooms, where Shelley drank a little too much to calm her nerves, they adjourned to the sofa for a kiss and a cuddle before Edward showed her to her bedroom. This was Andrew's room next to his and there was an inviting connecting door between the two. Alas, the door stayed firmly shut the entire night. Edward was a confusing mixture of good manners and shyness, so both of them spent the entire night gazing at the ceiling, ears pricked for a sound of the other stirring. Who knows what might have happened had Shelley been as forward as the Balmoral maid and boldly entered the Prince's sleeping quarters. But she did not and there was to be no night of unbridled passion. Instead, Edward kissed her goodbye the next morning and courteously arranged for her to be driven to the station. Although nothing happened on that evening, two stories subsequently showed that the teenagers had a very close physical relationship whether they actually did the deed or not. First, on one occasion at Balmoral they were both chatting outside the stables when they suddenly disappeared into an empty stall. A member of the staff witnessed this and was intrigued to know where they had gone so he went to investigate. Following sounds of rustling and squealing, he discovered the youngsters enjoying a lusty snog in the hayloft. The second incident happened at the Windsor Horse Show when a photographer saw Edward and Shelley disappear into stables where a sign on the door stated PRIVATE - KEEP OUT so, in the best Fleet Street tradition, he barged straight in and discovered them in each other's arms. 'Oh, terribly sorry,' said the photographer innocently and walked out. He had seen enough.

As far as a proper boy-girl relationship goes, Edward cut his teeth on Shelley, a very nice, ordinary girl who was fond of him. They went out together for almost two years, but without seeing a great deal of one another. If there was a party, Edward would invite Shelley. Coincidentally Shelley went to the same school as Edward's favourite photographer Jayne Fincher who recalls: 'My sister was a hairdresser and she used to do Shelley's hair. We always knew when she was going somewhere special because she used to come and get her hair done.' Sadly but inevitably their relationship fizzled out. In the cold light of day Shelley was too far downstairs and Edward too far upstairs for their friendship to develop, but they kept in touch and, having given up the world of horses, Shelley is now happily settled working as a doctor's receptionist in Surrey. Like Edward, she is still single.

Edward has never gone in for public courtships. When he has felt safe and secure he has been able to relax in the company of the opposite sex. He was popular with the girls during his year in New Zealand where he perfected his chat-up line, which was to ask a young lady to guess the colour of his eyes. They would inevitably declare them to be blue whereupon he would encourage a much closer inspection so that they could see that the corner of his left eye was green. The theatre once again drew him to a girl called Alison Bell who worked for a local radio station in Wanganui. They appeared together in an amateur production of the farce *Charley's Aunt* and afterwards Edward grabbed her for a surprise kiss. 'He has lovely soft lips,' purred Alison before adding, 'He is definitely not shy with girls.' Alison observed that Edward was happier entertaining girls with witty jokes than 'laughing with the boys'.

At Cambridge Edward was the soul of discretion, as he had to be with the lenses of the paparazzi trained on his every move in case he was seen with a young woman. During his very first term, Sir Alan Cottrell, the Master of Jesus College, complained twice to the Press Council about the treatment dished out to fellow student Corinne Taylor. She and Edward were appearing together in the college production of *The Crucible* when two and two were put together to make five and the word went out that they were an item. Corinne lived in a house at the side of the college, which was overlooked by a multi-storey car park. The photographers camped out on the top floor with their camera lenses focused on her bedroom just in case Edward showed. Sir Alan told Ingrid Seward that it was 'intolerable for the poor girl who was only about 20' and he had to arrange for her to live in the college itself for her own peace of mind. This was one bad example and served as a warning to the young prince that discretion would always be essential if he was to enjoy any normal relationships. He was able secretly to enjoy the company of a number of women, but nothing serious developed. As Royal expert Margaret Holder astutely points out: 'He is like a number of young men who wait until they fall in love and find the right person before embarking on a sexual relationship.'

During his time at Cambridge he embarked on what was easily the most 'sexual' relationship so far with a girl. And what a girl. Romy Adlington was 17 and beautiful. The slender brunette, whose family lived in Micheldever in Hampshire, first made Edward's eyes pop out at the Royal Yacht Squadron Ball during Cowes Week in the summer of 1983. Just two nights later they met again at the Royal London Yacht Club and Edward latched on to her for the entire evening. They formed a very close relationship over the next two years and, although it might be stretching a point to say that Romy broke the Prince's heart, he met her a boy and parted from her a man having learnt a thing or two about the female sex along the way. At the Royal London, Edward impetuously asked her to join him at Balmoral whereupon Romy did the one thing guaranteed to inflame the passion of a potential suitor — she declined. She was carving out a career for herself as a promising young model and had a number of assignments lined up in London that she could not cancel. However, not many girls would turn down an invitation to Balmoral. The rejected Edward started to pursue Romy like a demented moth around a flame. He phoned, he wrote, he issued invitations left, right and centre until she eventually agreed to join him for a night at the theatre followed by supper at Buckingham Palace. Supper, as Romy later revealed, merged into breakfast served in bed by a valet while Edward's collection of teddy bears looked on disapprovingly.

It dawned on Romy that Edward had meticulously planned her seduction. First, there was supper wheeled into Edward's suite on a trolley by a liveried servant. There was beef and vegetables served in impressive silver dishes and a bottle of claret. Romy clutched a glass of wine and settled down in front of the fire to let the romantic setting wash over her. They talked for ages while Edward plucked up the courage to pounce on this dream girl. Romy observed: 'It was obvious he was not used to having girlfriends spend the night with him.' In the bedroom, which was to one side of his sitting-room, they lay on one of the two single beds and talked for hours before passion got the better of them.

Eventually they fell asleep in each other's arms just before dawn only to be woken almost immediately by a valet bringing in Edward's early-morning cuppa. The breakfast tray was laid for two, which made Romy think the staff had been briefed in advance. She later recalled: 'Edward looked at me with what I can describe only as amused conquest. I think he felt quite proud that he could have a girlfriend to stay the night with him, right under his mother's nose. The Queen was in residence and I don't think she would have liked to know I was tucked up in bed with her youngest son.' That may or may not have been the case, but her overnight stay set an early precedent that certainly made things easier for Sophie. 'We were both young and inexperienced,' said Romy, 'in a way that was quite sweet.' Subsequent stories about their affair, including the serialisation of Romy's account in the *Sunday Mirror*, have suggested that Edward was a virgin before that night, but that was not the case.

That night Romy had to run a gauntlet familiar to all young women who 'stay over'. She had to make her way home in the morning wearing what was obviously an evening frock. In Romy's case this was doubly difficult because it was Buckingham Palace and there were masses of people up and about preparing for an official luncheon that the Queen was giving. She had to march past everyone convinced they knew what she had been up to a few hours earlier. Edward, in wonderfully Royal fashion, gave her a peck on the cheek and said: 'Thank you so much for last night.'

Over the next 18 months or so, Romy's life mirrored the early courtship of Edward and Sophie. She stayed at Windsor, Sandringham, Balmoral and at Wood Farm on the Norfolk Estate where they could be less formal. Most weekends they went away but Edward, already displaying the desire for privacy that Sophie quickly discovered, would go to great lengths to maintain secrecy. He would always travel under an alias and Romy would go along with his ruses because they were fun. On one memorable occasion they went out to dinner in London with Edward wearing a cunning disguise. Romy remembered: 'We built up his nose, greased his hair back, added sideburns and gave him a wonderful moustache, stuck on with glue. We thought we had got away with it until the end of the meal, but just as we were being served coffee Edward leant across the table and his moustache caught fire on the candle. It frazzled away completely except for a bit in the middle, which made it look like he was impersonating Adolf Hitler.'

Romy probably got on better with Edward's immediate family than any girlfriend until Sophie. Several years later she told the *Sunday Mirror* newspaper: 'The Queen was immediately friendly and charming. There was no snootiness or unpleasantness about her.' Romy described how she went shopping with Princess Anne and bought her a pair of Union Jack boxer shorts and how she cooked sausages on a barbecue while the Queen and Prince Philip bickered about the washing-up. She recalled how the Queen Mother had approached her on a bitterly cold morning's shooting and offered a snifter of sloe gin with the words,

'This will warm you up inside'. It was all good knock-about stuff and an insight into a life to come for Sophie. Romy's story was far from a kiss-and-tell revelation and was sympathetic to Edward, of whom she observed: 'He is very sensitive, which some people don't make allowances for.'

The problem for Edward and Romy was that they lived in different worlds. He was stuck at Cambridge trying to keep their romance going while she was moving in glamorous circles in London. Nor did it help that she had another boyfriend, a film director called Nick Hooper. It hit Edward hard when he realised he wanted more and she wanted less. She explained: 'He was looking for a really committed relationship, more of a commitment than I could give him at the time. I knew he was very upset, but I tried to explain that I wasn't ready to settle down. At the time I was travelling around the world as a model and simply couldn't give him the attention he needed.' It was a painful lesson for Edward, especially when she failed to turn up for a birthday party he had especially arranged for her and he had to phone her mother to find out where she was. Things did not get any better and the writing was on the wall for their relationship when Romy paid her last visit to Balmoral in the summer of 1985 and they both realised that their lives had moved on. In fact, Edward already had a replacement lined up according to Romy except that he made a mess of the timing (or should that be two-timing) and she turned up a day early. 'I was only just beginning to pick up some of the rules about etiquette', Romy said. 'This girl was obviously new to it and I could predict disaster. When she came in she made straight for a chair that nobody sits in. I think it was the one used by Queen Victoria. The poor girl didn't know, of course, but just as she went to sit down

Prince Charles grabbed her in mid-air and said "Sorry. Not that one". It summed up the whole other-worldly side of the Royal Family. They have a set of rules and codes of behaviour — rules that Edward knows and has been raised in.' Sophie would need to learn this rule book by heart.

Back at Cambridge Edward had formed an alliance with a sporty and spirited girl called Eleanor Weightman who became his best female chum there. They met at Cowes, which has always been a happy hunting-ground for Edward. Most of the girls with whom he has become involved are either sporty and keen on outdoor pursuits like sailing and riding or they are connected in some way with the media and the theatre. His ideal girl clearly would be one who could combine the two. One further essential quality was a sense of fun and the ability to laugh at the same things Prince Edward found amusing. All three ingredients in one woman would be like three oranges coming up on a fruit machine. Edward would often get two oranges, but he would have to wait until he met Sophie before he hit the jackpot. In Eleanor, however, he found a student soulmate. On the door of her college room hung a notice that stated: 'Appreciate me now — avoid the rush later,' which made Edward giggle every time he visited. The pair would have tea, study in the library and turn up to support each other's sporting endeavours. She would stand on the touchline to watch him get pummelled playing rugby and he would watch her play ice hockey, which is about the roughest sport around. He once rolled up to a late-night game at the Oxford ice rink, much to the surprise of Eleanor's team captain who remarked: 'Nobody could understand why he came — except he must like butch, sweaty women.'

Eleanor was just five feet tall so they made an odd

couple. Edward nicknamed her Munchkin after one of the minuscule characters from *The Wizard of Oz*. They shared affection and companionship, but lacked the spark of true love. Although they went skiing and he stayed at her parents' home in Cheshire, the truth is that they were just good pals. They remain in touch and Eleanor has never talked of those student days. Although Romy Adlington did speak to the *Sunday Mirror* several years later in 1990, at least she was complimentary and, so far, no one has planted a poison-edged knife between Edward's shoulder-blades.

9

Marine Psychology

hile Sophie was happily settling in to one of the most carefree periods of her life at Capital Radio, Edward was embarking on one of his unhappiest as an officer in the Royal Marines. With the benefit of hindsight it seems incredible that Edward should so nearly have been consigned to life as a commando. This is the man who loves the theatre and the company of the luvvies who inhabit it. He is a man who has loved every minute of his amateur acting career, including the dressing-up and the greasepaint. To think of Edward as a Marine is to imagine a member of the cast of *It Ain't Half Hot Mum* landing a role in *Terminator*. It comes as no surprise to learn that that classic television comedy has always been one of the Prince's favourites. So how on earth did it come about that, in September 1986 just three months after leaving Cambridge, he presented himself at the Marine HQ in Lympstone, Devon, to begin a full time commission?

*   *   *

Edward first forged a connection with the Royal Marines four years earlier in May 1992 when he enrolled for a potential officers' training course. His father and both his brothers had gone into the services and it has proved a tried and trusted Royal career route. Edward, always a stickler for protocol and tradition, was anxious to follow the correct path. He made this important decision while still a schoolboy embracing the Spartan atmosphere of Gordonstoun. He was mapping out a career path before he had tasted the freedom of nine months abroad in New Zealand and, perhaps more significantly, before he had absorbed the influences of Cambridge where he enjoyed himself so much. He had written to Romy Adlington telling her how great he thought university life. One of his commanding officers made a telling entry in his diary after Edward had undergone a week's intensive training: 'Splendid sense of humour, very alert and well read, with a worldliness beyond his years.' From intelligent discussion in his rooms at Jesus to mud-splattered assault training at the camp in Lympstone, Devon, proved a leap too far. The shock was that Edward had the courage to quit, not that he wanted to. For anyone who knows of Edward's sensitivity, there was no surprise in that.

Believe it or not, joining the Marines had been a boyhood dream rather like other youngsters dream of being engine drivers or astronauts. Edward, who loved James Bond films, pictured himself as a *Boy's Own* hero. His ambitions were also undoubtedly fuelled by a desire to match his father and brothers. He was a great deal closer to his father than many appreciated and did not welcome the suggestion that he was a mummy's boy.

Prince Philip was Captain General of the Marines, their overall ceremonial chief. Charles enjoyed the nickname Action Man, while Andrew was considered something of a hero for flying a Sea King helicopter during the Falklands War. Edward was merely 'Educated Eddie'. He wanted to prove he could be tough and there is nothing tougher than the physical and mental torture of training for the Royal Marines.

On his very first instruction weekend, Edward was woken in the middle of the night and bullied onto the assault course for a session, which ended with him being plunged into a tank of cold water. Marine Sergeant Taff Simmons, who was in charge of physical fitness, memorably said when he was told he would be in charge of the Prince: 'I'll run that little fucker off his feet, Sir.' Edward officially became a Second Lieutenant at the Commando Training Centre, Lympstone, in September 1982 just before flying out to Wanganui for his New Zealand idyll.

His first taste of the 'good life' in store for him as a Marine came soon after he had gone up to Cambridge. It was December 1983 and Edward spent a week on detachment in Belize with 40 Commando Royal Marines. This could have been taken straight out of an Oliver Stone movie. Belize, formerly British Honduras, would not be everyone's first choice as a holiday destination. Plagued by floods and hurricanes, nearly half the country is covered by trees and jungle. Edward's trip began with a quick introduction of how to survive in the jungle. He learnt how to sling a hammock off the ground, how to make a fire and put together a temporary shelter using a small tree and a groundsheet. So far so good, it was rather like an advanced scouting excursion.

Edward was told of the importance of navigation in

the jungle, because it is very easy to lose your bearings when you are completely surrounded by densely-covered trees. The do-it-yourself instruction was the easy part. Home for the next night was a 2ftx7ft trench, which Edward dug for himself. There is no way to make yourself comfortable in a trench, especially when it is boiling hot and humid and mosquitoes the size of rifle bullets are practising their dive-bombing techniques on your head. His comfortable bed at Buckingham Palace seemed a lifetime away.

Next day Edward was up and out into the jungle on river patrol, weighed down with pack, ammunition and rifle with his face blackened so the invisible enemy would not catch sight of his rosy cheeks. Edward, with the eyes of the other men on him, had to prove himself time and time again in this harsh environment. He had to show he was made of the 'right stuff'. It is faintly ridiculous that, having dragged his aching, insect-bitten body out of his jungle fatigues, he had to climb into black-tie formal evening wear for a dinner with the commander of the British forces in Belize. He would always be a Prince among the men. Ironically, the moment Edward finished training to be an élite fighting machine his faithful bodyguard Andrew Merrylees was back in position at his side.

*   *   *

On leaving Cambridge Edward threw himself into his first serious flurry of public engagements, including a trip to New Zealand to publicise the Duke of Edinburgh's Award scheme, which has continued to be his most important official pursuit. Just three days before he set out for Lympstone Barracks, he attended the Award's thirtieth anniversary ball at Broadlands —

the home of his murdered uncle, Lord Mountbatten. There was so much going on that particular summer that Edward barely had a chance to draw breath. If he had been given the opportunity to go away and quietly consider his future, he might never have made the trip to Devon. As it was he had to fit in the Queen's 60th birthday celebration, a period of family mourning following the death of the Duchess of Windsor and, of most consequence, be best man (or supporter as they called it) at the wedding of his brother Andrew to Sarah Ferguson in Westminster Abbey. In just ten years Fergie has wreaked havoc in the Royal world and put a great deal of pressure on Edward to make a better choice of a marriage partner. Edward looked happy and relaxed at the wedding, a dashing figure in the ceremonial dress uniform of the Royal Marines. He would have little use for it in the future unless he decided to wear it for a fancy dress party.

According to author Robin Eggar (a former *Sunday Mirror* journalist) in his book about the Marines entitled *Commando, Survival of the Fittest*, there comes a point where everyone, however physically fit and motivated, will want to give up. Just when Edward finally realised that his personal happiness was being threatened by his sense of duty remains unclear. It took him less than four months to appreciate that he had made a monumental mistake. But those few weeks were a complete nightmare. Marine Colonel Alan Hooper told Ingrid Seward: 'If you can do anything with your life why spend wet, miserable nights on Dartmoor unless you have to?'

Edward arrived at Lympstone on 7 September, 1986, one of 36 young officer recruits but the only Prince. He had the rank of Second Lieutenant, which was automatic for a graduate in the Marines University

Entrance Scheme and he was on the far from princely starting salary of £7,391 per year. His bodyguard installed Edward at one end of the barracks in a bedroom that, although a palace in comparison with a Belize trench, was only 12ftx10ft with not a Gainsborough in sight on its simple whitewashed walls. The bodyguard took the room next to him and made sure there were a number of empty rooms between his charge and the other young officers, or 'yo-yos' as service slang termed them.

The thought on everyone's minds was why Edward needed a middle-aged Special Branch man to protect him when he was surrounded by supremely fit fighting men who would lay down their lives for Queen and country. These living arrangements helped to erect a physical and mental barrier between Edward and his colleagues, something a man as reserved as Prince Edward would find impossible to overcome.

Although he can be the life and soul of the party, Edward relaxes only in the company of friends and those he trusts. The only saving grace was that two fellow yo-yos, Peter Fraser and Quintus Travis, had been at Cambridge with Edward. Fraser quit the Marines at the same time as Edward, while Travis won the Sword of Honour as the leading recruit.

Coping with the extreme physical demands of his training was, in the final analysis, much easier for Edward compared with the mental stress that manifested itself in the suppression of his individuality and freedom. It felt as though he was not allowed to think for himself. That is not to say that the physical side of things was not a challenge. Edward has always been an early riser and so a regular 6.00am start was not a problem. Unfortunately, there was no valet on hand to bring him a hot cup of tea and a digestive biscuit or to make sure his towels had been warmed overnight. Instead, there was early morning PE and weapons training. Then it was back to school for a series of classroom-based lessons complete with homework. Edward was 22 going on 23 when he faced the daunting challenge of the endurance course on Dartmoor. It began with a speed march, followed by a crawl through a pitch-black 30-foot-long tunnel and along a thin rope across a stretch of icy water known as 'Peter's Pool'. If you were still dry after that, next up was a 10ft-long concrete pipe filled with water. A speed march back to the barracks ended with just ten minutes to wash and brush up before the now spick-and-span recruit was on the parade ground.

Edward's commanding officer Colonel Ian Moore may have had cause to regret his statement about the Green Beret, the symbol of a Marine officer. 'It will not be handed to Prince Edward on a plate', he said. 'He will have to earn it.' Having Prince Edward as a serving officer was great publicity for the Marines and a golden opportunity to retain a high profile, which would be useful in fighting any defence cuts. Having the same Prince Edward quitting the service was a PR disaster.

Edward served only 12 weeks before breaking for Christmas, but during that time a couple of incidents preyed heavily on his mind and they helped to tip the scales in favour of resignation. First, there was the notorious 'Kiss' story. Edward is supposed to have been adjusting his cap in a mirror when a long-serving sergeant walked by. 'How do I look?' asked Edward casually, whereupon the sergeant replied, 'You look lovely, Sir, just lovely,' before sweeping Edward into his arms and giving him a big smacker on the cheek. He only just stopped short of calling Edward 'You lovely boy'. The story is now a Marine legend, albeit an unwelcome one. It is probably not true, but spread quicker than an outbreak of cholera. Here, it appeared, was a Prince and a lieutenant being publicly humiliated by a sergeant.

The second and more serious incident concerned the ramming of mud down Prince Edward's throat, a tasty treat that, it was said afterwards, many recruits have to endure. One afternoon Edward was watching a game of touch rugby on the muddy banks of the River Exe. He was slightly injured so was not playing and, along with three others, was standing on the 'touchline'. Suddenly the players decided that these four, and Edward in particular, were looking far too clean for their liking and set about getting them well and truly muddy. The incident is graphically described by fellow recruit, Lieutenant Matt Lodge, who says, 'They rammed mud in his ears, in his mouth, right up his nose and poured so much inside his shirt that he could have been Mud Pie Man.' Lt Lodge concludes that it was a coded warning to Edward to treat his equals with the respect they gave each other.

It is easy to imagine that the pompous and sometimes officious streak that Edward is prone to display from time to time would rub these fighting men up the wrong way. Robin Eggar claimed that the other young officers regarded Edward as a prima donna who would bellow orders like a drill sergeant shouting at first-day recruits. Like many naturally shy people, Edward was liable to go right over the top when given a position of authority.

The mud incident was regarded by Colonel Moore as a 'skylark' and Edward never complained, but he would have needed a heart of stone not to be affected. And the sensitive Prince does not have a heart of stone. He could presumably have joined his tormentors for a pint of aftershave in the local pub, but instead he trudged back to barracks, crestfallen and covered in mud from head to toe. As he tried to slip anonymously into the officers' mess a young recruit saluted him. Eggar, who spent 15 months with the Royal Marines while researching his book — 12 months longer than Edward managed — says of the incident: 'The message to Edward was received and understood but instead of getting tough, the Prince got going.'

As usual, Christmas was spent at Sandringham among friends and family. Edward spent much of it absorbed in his own dilemma, the classic confrontation between personal happiness and a sense of duty. In the Services they refer to this as the 'wobbles', a time to question whether one could face five more years of something so unfulfilling. The terms of Edward's commission meant he would be a Marine for a minimum of five years or, put another way, for most of his twenties.

Edward had dinner with Romy Adlington and poured his heart out to the girl who had always been such a sympathetic listener. For the first time he admitted outside the family group that he did not want to go back to the Marines. He drove to Cambridge to discuss his predicament with his former tutor, Dr Gavin Mackenzie, who firmly told him to get out of the Marines. In no way did this saga become a case of Edward defying the wishes of his mother and father. The Queen and Prince Philip are both infused with an enormous sense of duty and Edward is well aware of the priorities in Royal life. However, he is the Queen's youngest son and will never be king. His parents would never knowingly wish him to be unhappy, although they did suggest he take more time to consider his decision. By the time the bells rang in the

New Year Edward had made up his mind not to return to Lympstone. His New Year Resolution was immovable. It was yet another indication that, although Edward can dither about a decision, once he has made it he sticks to it. It is a characteristic that Sophie has come to know well, as she has watched him resist all outside pressures on him to marry her, making the decision in his own time.

Edward was due to return to his barracks on Monday, 5 January. His group known as Young Officers Batch 86, which made them sound like battery chickens, were to ease back into the routine with a route march across Dartmoor in sub-zero temperatures. Fortunately Edward had a sick note from the Palace, which said he had flu and would be staying in London for a few days. Edward spent the day composing his letter of resignation.

The next day Sir Michael Watkins, Edward's Commanding Officer, who had been informed of the problem by Prince Philip, went to the Palace to try to persuade him to change his mind. He was the first of many to try and fail, although Edward agreed to travel to Lympstone the following morning to talk with his fellow officers. Obviously the thinking was that Edward was more likely to reconsider if he was back at the barracks.

Before he set out on the 300-mile journey he was greeted by headlines in the daily papers. Someone had leaked to the *Sun* a private letter from Prince Philip to Sir Michael Watkins revealing Edward's intention to resign from the Marines. The Press became like gold prospectors sifting through every granule searching for a nugget. It seemed like the world and his wife had an opinion on Edward's dilemma. His university tutor even appeared on the Jimmy Young radio programme.

Meanwhile Edward kept his promise to return to Lympstone where he was counselled for two hours by officers who hoped he would decide to stay on. Eventually he agreed to sleep on it for a few days and let everyone know his final decision after the weekend, which, with a twist of irony, he ended up spending shooting at Wood Farm next to Sandringham.

The Press were having a field day. They discovered that his best friend in the Marines, Peter Fraser, was also resigning. He said that he thought Edward was leaving because 'three years of university had broadened his horizons'. The newspapers preferred the explanation that Edward had found the training too tough. They gleefully reported that he had been accident prone, injuring his ankle and knee and getting a black eye in a boxing match with another marine. It was also said that he had 'wept' for three hours before finally deciding to resign.

That resignation formally came on the Monday as promised. He travelled to Lympstone for the last time and suffered the excruciating embarrassment of saying goodbye to his fellow officers. It was a difficult afternoon and when Edward drove off there was more relief than regret on all sides. When he got back to the Palace, Edward proceeded to get well and truly sozzled.

About a third of all trainees quit the Marines so there is no reason why Edward should not do so. Buckingham Palace issued what was for them quite a loquacious statement: 'After much consideration HRH Prince Edward has decided to resign from the Royal Marines. An announcement about his future plans is not expected for some time. Prince Edward is leaving the Marines with great regret but has decided that he does not wish to make the service his long-term career.'

The *New York Post* reacted to the news by calling

Edward 'The Weeping Wimp of Windsor', which has the merit of being alliterative but nothing more. Royal biographer Anthony Holden sensibly suggested that Edward 'had merely had the good sense to question the value of a military career. He has shown that he wishes to be his own man and thus choose his own career, not have it chosen for him, nor to live his life merely by tradition or precedent.' For once, the nation seemed to agree with a decision that a member of the Royal Family had made — in a specially commissioned poll for the *Sunday Express* 80 per cent supported the Prince.

It would be some years before Edward felt able to share his feelings about leaving the Marines. For the moment he had the backing of his family who closed ranks behind him. A few days after his resignation he walked side by side with his father to church at Sandringham.

It was a gesture that told the public that Prince Philip was on his son's side. Although Edward opened his heart to friends about his reasons for leaving and the mental anguish his decision caused him, he did not speak about it publicly for some eight years until he finally admitted to Ingrid Seward that at the time he knew he was never going to be able to fit in as a Marine. 'It was nothing against the Marines *per se* — it would have been the same across the board in any of the Services. I could never go out with the rest of the lads into the town because everybody knew who I was. It was always obvious you were a Royal Marine because everybody had short haircuts. And I would always have a policeman with me. I was never going to fit in as I had envisaged and that more than anything else decided me.'

At the Royal Tournament later that year, the 100 or so members of Yankee Company 45 Commando wore special T-shirts — on the front was the message 'You can turn a frog into a Prince' ... On the back it read '... but you can't turn a Prince into a Marine'. Others wore T-shirts declaring 'I have gone where princes fear to tread'. If Prince Edward ever had doubts about the wisdom of his decision, then recalling these examples of wit must surely have made him realise it was the best decision he ever made.

10

More Hard Knocks

The world, it seems, often caught the young Prince Edward by surprise. He had the unfortunate knack of rushing head down into a china shop and then appearing astonished when he ended up smashing plates. As the youngest son he has been indulged and protected so he has not always been equipped to temper his enthusiasm with common street savvy. And so, ludicrously, the *It's A Royal Knock-Out* fiasco in the summer of 1987 made a far more lasting impression on the general public than the trauma of his short-lived career in the Royal Marines. It also sheds some light on Edward's mistrust of the Press, and why he will go to such elaborate lengths to maintain his privacy. He is not alone among his family in mishandling the Press, but the events of this rainy day in June proved to be a hard lesson. Like many an England cricket team, Edward contrived to snatch defeat from the jaws of victory.

The Grand Charity Knockout Tournament, as it was officially titled, must have seemed like a great idea in the pub but that is perhaps where it should have stayed. Edward conceived the idea with his old university friend Tim Hastie-Smith who later in his role as a clergyman was to give Edward important counsel about marrying Sophie. Edward had always been a fan of the BBC show *It's A Knock-Out* ever since, as an impressionable 13-year-old, he had mingled with the crowd at a day's filming in Windsor Great Park. His liking for the show, a by-word for kitsch entertainment, is thoroughly in keeping with his tastes for James Bond films, Abba and amateur dramatics. *It's A Knock-Out* was as 1970s as Slade, Suzi Quatro and outrageous platform shoes. By the time of the mid-1980s it was past its sell-by date and came across as childish. Members of the public were dressed up in silly costumes to take part in what were little more than party games for the under-tens. Banana skins and custard pie japes are just not that funny. As actor Christopher Reeve, alias Superman, put it: 'The first question that crossed my mind when I was asked to participate was just how silly was silly?' Very silly indeed, proved to be the answer.

Edward threw himself into its organisation with the same gusto and enthusiasm that had marked his efforts in light entertainment at Cambridge. He was only 23, which is worth remembering when sitting in final judgement, and could be forgiven for picturing himself as a great impresario. He meticulously set about the massive task of co-ordinating the day, as if it were a giant school project. Edward found sponsors, accountants, solicitors and PR people. He sat down with BBC producers and worked out every minute detail of the show, including all the props, costumes and even camera angles. The photographer Jayne Fincher was on the organising committee with him and is full of praise for his efforts, a view that suggests the Royal Marines were the losers when Edward left the service. She recalls: 'We met up every week for six months and he was totally different to how I thought he would be. You always get the impression that he is quite pompous, but when you work with him that is not the case. He was not at all stand-offish and was happy to be one of the team. He trusted the people he was working with and felt relaxed in their company.

'The committee were all young people drawn from a wide field. Tim Hastie-Smith was at Cambridge with Edward, James Baker was one of his closest friends and Abel Hadden knew him well so it was very friendly. There were representatives from the BBC and from the accountants. Edward was in charge of everything and what surprised me was what a good leader he was, without being bossy. He was an excellent motivator and good at getting the right people together. What I found particularly fascinating was how artistic he was. He did a lot of sketches himself of how he envisaged the set and costumes. I think the BBC were quite impressed by him, too. I think this is probably where he first got a flavour of television. He was very meticulous even down to costume details, which he would check thoroughly with the wardrobe department.'

Jayne was on good terms with Edward because she was a riding chum of his old girlfriend Shelley Whitborn, who mentioned her to the Prince one day. The next time Edward saw Jayne she was taking pictures at the Windsor Horse Show and Edward gallantly went up and opened the door of the Press Range Rover for her and remarked, 'We've got a mutual friend.' Jayne is very down-to-earth, just like Sophie in some ways, and so she and Edward have always got along well and attended many official events together. She has always found Edward to be good-humoured, easy to work with and 'unstuffy'. Illustrating that point she says, 'He remembered the names of everyone on the committee and called us all by our first names. I never called him Prince Edward or Edward. I just used to say Sir but some of them just called him Edward because it was all very casual. Edward often made the tea himself, which highlighted how informal everything was. I was impressed by how approachable he was.'

Edward and his committee decided on Alton Towers in Staffordshire as the venue and chose the theme for the day. Prompted by Edward they settled on setting the entire event 400 years ago in 1587, the year before the Spanish Armada when Elizabeth I was on the throne. This would allow everyone to dress up in Tudor costumes. Edward would wear a yellow costume complete with yellow hat and plumed feather and bright yellow stockings, which made him look like an image on a playing card. *The Times* described him as looking like 'one of Shakespeare's lesser jesters'.

Since that day Edward has had a horror of being pictured looking foolish in fancy dress. This explains why he blew his top when a photograph of him and Sophie Rhys-Jones in fancy dress appeared on the front cover of *Hello!* magazine in the autumn of 1996. The occasion was the 70th birthday ball of Lord Montagu of Beaulieu where guests were invited to interpret the Shakespearean theme of 'If Music Be The Food Of Love Play On'. Sophie looked prim as a 12th-century knight (or Twelfth Knight) whereas Edward wore a sort of white tabard covered in Shakespearean verses, which looked more like a peculiar night-dress. He had, *Hello!* informed us, sewn it himself.

*   *   *

Edward's fashion sense really needs taking in hand.
During the rehearsals for *Knock-Out* he wore a T-shirt
that proclaimed 'No, I just look like him', which hinted
at a self-mockery the average member of the public does
not want to see in the Royal Family. The most amusing
exchange came at a Press conference when he was asked
if he had signed a contract with the BBC. Edward
grinned and replied, tongue firmly in cheek, 'The only
thing I've signed was a piece of paper promising not to
get married this year.' His elder brother had, of course,
married Sarah Ferguson the previous year at great
expense to the nation. It would turn out to be ten years
before Edward was ready to get married.

*   *   *

The idea for the day's festivities was that members of the
Royal Family would captain four teams of celebrities in a
series of 'knock-out' games, each team supporting a
particular charity. Edward opted for his favourite, The
Duke of Edinburgh's Award Scheme. Princess Anne
represented the Save the Children Fund, the Duke of York
went for The Worldwide Fund for Nature and his
boisterous wife the International Year of Shelter. They
were all very worthy causes. Prince Charles and Princess
Diana sensibly steered well clear. Edward's Royal
prestige and powers of persuasion, however, attracted an
array of some 50 international names, all of whom he had
contacted personally. His own team consisted of Dame
Kiri Te Kanawa, Nicholas Lyndhurst, John Cleese, Toyah
Wilcox and sports personalities Barry McGuigan, Duncan
Goodhew, Tessa Sanderson and Steve Cram. Prince

Andrew's team included John Travolta, Michael Palin, Griff Rhys-Jones (no relation to Sophie), former James Bond George Lazenby, Anneka Rice and sportsmen Nigel Mansell and Gary Lineker. Fergie's team comprised Jane Seymour, Mel Smith, Chris De Burgh, Pamela Stephenson, Ben Cross, Michael Brandon, Meatloaf, cricket legend Viv Richards and jockey Steve Cauthen. Princess Anne lined up with Anthony Andrews, Cliff Richard, Tom Jones, Jenny Agutter, Sheena Easton, Jackie Stewart and Emlyn Hughes. You would be hard pushed to get that many stars at the Oscars. Unlike the Academy Awards where the stars put on their most glittering outfits, here on a rainy, damp day at Alton Towers they had to don a motley collection of Tudor costumes. Anthony Andrews summed up the bewilderment of the Hollywood contingent when he observed, 'One could see quite clearly that it was slowly dawning on their jet-lagged brains just how silly they were about to look.' The judge for the day was magician Paul Daniels who, unfortunately was unable to make the entire thing disappear. Presiding over the proceedings like a demented jack-in-the-box was Stuart Hall, the host of the television series. John Travolta unintentionally hit the bull's eye when he said, 'This seems so typically English'.

Monday 15 June, 1987, was a day without dignity. Torrential rain turned Alton Towers into a huge mud pie, which, in view of his Marines' torture, was not Edward's preferred underfoot conditions. Even Edward admitted, 'Looking out the window at the torrential rain that morning was the worst moment of my life.' Luckily for them the four Royal team captains had not been given permission by the Queen to take part in the games, although Fergie seemed to be everywhere.

Her all-neighing all-braying performance had to be seen to be believed. At the eve of tournament banquet, she set the tone by hurling after-dinner mints at her husband. On the day of the competition itself, she pelted him with apples, oranges and pears. She was, we were assured, suffering from laryngitis.

The silliness of the day might have been swallowed by all and sundry if Edward, or whoever was advising him, had not decided to treat the Press like second-class citizens. Although many people might think that is several classes too high, it is a fact of life that it is better to have them with you than against you. The Press were banned from the site and the efforts of some 50 journalists to sneak into the main arena failed. Instead, they were herded into a pen outside the security fence and forced to watch some ten hours of mind-boggling inane 'fun' on television with no bar and no prospect of getting a decent story for their papers. Only Jayne Fincher was allowed to take photographs, the idea being that these could be sold to increase the profits for the charities involved, which was the point of the day. Even Andrew Morton, then a reporter on the *Daily Star*, could not cajole a pass for himself despite his paper buying exclusive rights to the photos. 'He hasn't forgiven me to this day', says Jayne. 'Andrew said to me, "You know I work for the *Star* and we have bought the pictures so I must be able to come in." But I said, "No, you can't." I said to Prince Edward, "You know what's going to happen. They're going to get dressed up in costumes and hide their cameras up their knickerbockers." I told him we needed those security things that you walk through at Heathrow Airport and he said, "Leave it to me, I'll get them," and that's what we did. I had to hide from all the photographers. I thought they were going to kill me.'

The irony was that photos were available to everyone provided they paid £1,000 or so for the privilege, but no one was prepared to do that believing they would get photographs for themselves. Jayne Fincher, who knew all the tricks, was not going to let them. So a swell of resentment built up in the press tent. Unfortunately, Edward was unable to grasp the enormity of the hole he had dug for himself. At the end of the day he arrived at a Press tent full of malcontents. They had missed their deadlines, had been unable to see a thing and now had to listen to Prince Edward who, forgetting none of them had seen it, expected them to tell him how wonderful the day had been. Near the end of a boring prepared speech he paused for breath and the ITN reporter, the late Joan Thirkettle, jumped in to ask if he was pleased with the way everything had gone. 'I haven't finished yet,' said Edward tetchily, little realising he was like a curious gazelle inspecting a tiger's toothache. He finished up by saying, 'I know the captains have enjoyed themselves. I only hope you have enjoyed yourselves — have you?' The silence was deafening and the exhausted young Prince took great umbrage. He stormed, 'Well, thanks for being so bloody enthusiastic. What have you been doing here all day?' Joan Thirkettle echoed the sentiments of every journalist there with the response: 'You may well ask.' Edward, with the tiger's jaws now firmly round his head, went on: 'Have you been watching it? What did you think?' He was greeted by the sound of guffaws and sniggers. It was too much for the proud young Prince who stormed to his feet. 'Thanks,' he said petulantly and marched out. The tigers of the Press were now asking for toothpicks. Edward's tantrum was a story on a plate and they gladly took it. Andrew Morton described Edward's performance: 'He flounced out like a ballerina with a hole in his tights.'

He went back to the headquarters muttering, 'I can't

understand them.' Everyone could see how upset he was and Jayne Fincher made him a cup of tea to help calm him down. He was still walking on eggshells when he was met by a posse of Press photographers as he left Alton Towers. 'One of these days you people are going to have to learn some manners', he declared, echoing the time he had warned Bryan Rostron 'this time I won't do what I could do to you'. Lynda Lee-Potter of the *Daily Mail* wrote that journalists had not hung around all day 'for the privilege of being sneered at by a rudely offensive young man.' Edward is not as foolish as these incidents make him appear. As soon as his anger had cooled, he realised he had shot himself and the entire day in the foot. He had given the Press a story and they did not shirk the issue when the next day's headlines proclaimed: ITS' A WALK-OUT.

Just how much damage this sorry affair did to the Royal Family is impossible to quantify, but dignity is a commodity that once lost is difficult to restore. Jayne Fincher is adamant that *It's A Royal Knock-Out* should not be the scapegoat for the Royal Family's ills and the committee still get fed up with all the criticism years later. After the event Edward would have the monumental task of convincing the world he was not a spoilt brat. Years later he is still very defensive. When Ingrid Seward suggested to him that it was 'disastrous', he bridled and replied, 'It wasn't disastrous. How can you call something disastrous that raised over a million pounds for charity?' That may be, but if Edward had gone to the Queen and asked her to write a cheque for a million pounds to stop her family from being perceived as a pack of buffoons, albeit unfairly, she probably would have thought it a cheap price to pay. In reality she had little idea of what was going on until it was too late.

It was time for Edward to start afresh.

11

Girls, Girls, Girls (II)

Cowes Week has always been a happy hunting-ground for Edward. As a Prince you are always likely to stumble across a promising lass wearing a nice frock at one of the numerous yachting club balls. He had met Romy Adlington and Eleanor Weightman there and now it was the turn of Georgia May, who probably came closer than anyone to marrying Edward until Sophie came along. In many ways Georgia is quite similar in looks and character to Sophie. It was at the Royal Yacht Squadron Ball in the summer of 1986 that she marched up to the Prince and asked him to dance. It certainly grabbed Edward's attention — not to mention that of the girl he was with and of Georgia's own escort. It worked though, and she and Edward bopped happily together much to the surprise of the man from the *Daily Express* who had gatecrashed the ball and to whom an ingenuous Georgia gushed afterwards, 'We just danced and danced. I had a wonderful time.'

Edward liked Georgia instantly. She was a strong-minded, no-nonsense girl, but he had the more pressing matter of the Royal Marines weighing on his mind for the coming months, although they kept in touch. As a Royal girlfriend, Georgia had plenty going for her. Over the next two years they enjoyed many times together, sailing with friends or riding in the grounds of Windsor or Sandringham. As a houseguest, Georgia's main claim to fame came the morning she darted up behind Prince Charles as he was helping himself to scrambled eggs, slapped him on the bottom and chirped, 'Morning, Chuck'. Charles, who has the sense of humour of a cold haddock, responded, 'Don't ever do that again,' leaving one to wonder if he was more upset at the hand on the Royal backside or being addressed as Chuck.

Georgia's father David (known as Daisy) is the millionaire owner of a boat company in the picturesque town of Lymington on the Hampshire coast. She lived with her mother in Fulham and pursued a career as a financial adviser. Georgia settled in to being Edward's steady girlfriend. Judy Wade, the Royal reporter for *Hello!* and one of the most knowledgeable observers of the Queen and her family, remembers going to see Georgia at her Fulham home: 'I knocked and she opened the door and, as we started to talk, the phone rang. It was exactly 5.30pm and she ran to that phone as only a woman in love does when she is expecting a call from her boyfriend. She didn't say, "Excuse me", she was just gone and I thought then "This girl is crazy about him".'

Everything seemed rosy but for one enormous problem — Georgia, just 21, was subjected to intense press investigation and speculation. It made Edward despair of any future relationships. The killer blow came when her father was revealed in a national newspaper as sharing a Docklands 'love-nest' not with Georgia's mother Catherine, a Belgian-born countess, but with a good-looking male accountant 18 years his junior. It is too simplistic to say, 'Who cares?' The tabloids would never ignore a scandal like this and poor Georgia began to hate the spotlight and scrutiny. EDWARD GIRL'S DAD IS A GAY proclaimed the *News of the World*. Georgia admitted candidly, 'All this attention is terrifying me.' If she found it disturbing after such a short time, how was she going to cope with it for a lifetime? Any lingering prospect of her being asked to find out disappeared when a former boyfriend spilled the beans on their romance and effectively lowered the curtain on her affair with Edward.

In many ways, Georgia was a dry run for the more important love affair with Sophie. Like Sophie, Georgia spent a New Year at Sandringham and enjoyed discreet country weekends with Edward and his friends. She was tipped as his future bride, even several months after they stopped dating. Judy Wade recalls that many Royal journalists expected an engagement announcement, just as everyone has spent many months anticipating formal news that he would marry Sophie. 'Georgia was a really nice, sweet girl, too,' says Judy. 'She and Sophie are quite similar except that Georgia comes from a wealthier background. They are both quite attractive with shortish hair. There is a type of girl that Edward likes and it is interesting that they are the sort of girls you wouldn't particularly look twice at in the street. They are not stunning. I thought she was crazy about Edward and it was getting serious, but he dropped her. OK, her father is gay, but is that a reason to drop a girl you really love?'

Georgia's time with Edward definitely came too early in her life. Coincidentally she is the same age as

Sophie, who probably would have coped no better if she had met Edward when she was just 21. As Georgia's father shrewdly observed: 'They are far too young to get married. She is getting cross at the media interest — she might crack.' Edward also showed signs of extreme touchiness, even vetoing any personal questions when he appeared on a children's chat show on Australian television. One ten-year-old girl who was primed to ask him, 'When are you getting married, Your Royal Highness?' was told in no uncertain terms to keep her hand down. Edward was right to do this, of course, because whatever harmless reply he gave would have reached the ears of the newspapers back home.

In the end, it was left to Georgia's mother Catherine to pour a bucket of cold water over the continuing fevered speculation about her daughter and Edward. She pleaded: 'I wish people would believe me. Georgia is not having an affair with Prince Edward. She did go out with him, but that has finished now. The romance is over. Why don't people get the message? The whole episode has been deeply upsetting for all involved. I am so upset at seeing all my family background on show to the British public. Why should the private lives of my family be on public display because Georgia went out with a Prince? Furious is not the word for the way I feel at the moment.'

It was a hard lesson for everyone involved, not least for Edward who privately told friends he would not wish being his girlfriend on his worst enemy. Edward resolved to protect his privacy and that of any future girlfriend with doubled vigour. The problem for Edward is that he has no control over the antics of the other members of the Royal Family, yet he will suffer the consequences of their actions. Indiscreet television appearances and lurid headlines put the entire clan under a powerful spotlight from which there is no place to hide. As he is the last of the Queen's children to marry, Edward has only to give a girl a second glance for her to be choosing her wedding dress in the eyes of the Press. For her part Georgia May, a highly sensible and motivated girl, got on with her life away from the public gaze. Her career as a financial adviser with Merrill Lynch prospered and she is now a married woman.

A classic way to divert attention from an affair is to step into the limelight with a new escort. Edward's closest pal James Baker, the son of broadcaster Richard Baker, was working at TVam back in 1987 and he told the Prince about a Swedish girl who had just joined the station as a junior secretary. Her name was Ulrika Jonsson and she was, he assured Edward, the tastiest export from Sweden since the smorgasbord. Edward's real girlfriend at that time was Georgia, with whom he never appeared in public. He did, however, roll up to the Henley Regatta Ball with Ulrika, who would make any photographer's lens mist over and who had journalists everywhere reaching for the 'blonde bombshell' book of clichés. Inevitably they were pictured together at Henley, even though James Baker and another girl were also there.

Ulrika had no idea when she set off for the evening that Edward was going to be joining them. 'James said he was going to the Henley Ball and didn't have a partner. I'd never been to a ball and had to borrow a dress from my Mum. James said we could change on the way and we drove to Windsor and then turned into the Castle. The police waved us through and my chin hit the floor. Then there was Edward walking over to us. I couldn't believe it. Then I remember sitting on the lawn, having a glass of Pimms with the Prince and watching the corgis. Thank God James never told me he was one of Edward's best friends. I would have bolted.' Ulrika had a couple of dates with Edward, including a trip to the West End to see *Three Men and a Horse* at the Vaudeville Theatre. The temporary liaison suited both their purposes very well. It gave Edward wonderful 'street cred' to be seen with a stunning 19-year-old Swedish girl and it won Ulrika the eye of the public. She did not waste it and gave an interview to a Stockholm newspaper in which she confessed, 'The hullabaloo that followed the news that we had been out together frightened me a little.' She spoke of picnics and the theatre and revealed that he visited her flat in Maida Vale, North London, always with his bodyguard present. Her mother said she and Edward were just friends and added, 'I don't think the Prince would consider marrying her,' which was quite true.

When she next arrived for work at the TVam studios in Camden, North London, Ulrika was besieged by the Press and left the offices lying face down in a Mercedes, which was good knock-about fun. It was the start of the rise and rise of Ulrika, the daughter of a Stockholm driving instructor, who went from secretary to weather girl, to presenter of *Gladiators*, to panellist on the brilliantly funny *Shooting Stars*, which has given her unexpected cult status. Her active private life has received the sort of attention that would have had Georgia May reaching for the smelling salts. Intriguingly she was the very first girl Edward had been seen with in public. As those that knew him realised, if she had been important he would have kept her as hidden as possible. It is one of the most telling aspects of his affair with Sophie that there are no more than a handful of photos of them together, even after nearly five years of courtship. Even quite recently, at a weekend shooting party at Sandringham, he smuggled Sophie in by a side door while his nephew Prince Harry and Charles's personal assistant Tiggy Legge-Bourke were happy and relaxed in front of photographers out the front.

Smuggling is a good word to describe Prince Edward's attitude to girls he likes. They are the contraband and the Press are the customs officers. If he goes through the 'Something to Declare' red channel as he did with Ulrika Jonsson, then it is almost certainly a bluff. If, however, he hurries through the 'Nothing to Declare' green channel, then he should be speedily apprehended for a thorough search. Take for instance the delightful television journalist Anastasia Cook who also worked for TVam. She was happily photographed with Edward in the red channel when it was quite clear to anyone who knew the situation that she was really James Baker's girlfriend all along. They are now married and remain among Edward's closest friends.

The cooling of Edward's relationship with Georgia May coincided with the beginning of an exciting new period in his life as a production assistant with Andrew Lloyd Webber's Really Useful Group, which had offices above the Palace Theatre. After his first day he returned home to the real 'Palace' and flopped into a chair next to the Queen who naturally asked him how it had all gone. Edward allegedly sighed, 'My God, I'm tired. You have no idea what a 10-hour day in the theatre is like.' The Queen is said to have replied, 'Yes, I have. I've been to the Royal Variety Performance.' The job was great publicity for everyone but was a very low rung on a long ladder for the ambitious Prince. It was at least a happy time because at long last he was embarking on a career he really wanted. Best of all he was mixing with a theatre crowd and he loved it. It would be stretching a point to say that Edward was the office boy, but actress Debbie Arnold, who played Carol Jackson's sister April in *EastEnders* remembers when she went for an interview and was told that 'Edward will meet you at the lift.' She was astonished when it turned out to be *Prince* Edward. 'He took me into an office and politely asked, "Would you like a cup of tea?" I couldn't believe it. A Royal was waiting on me! He was charming.'

Around this time Edward was escorting a pretty Welsh brunette called Rhian-Anwen Roberts. Anwen, as she was known to her friends, was studying English at Fitzwilliam College, Cambridge. She had been introduced to the Prince when he had gone back to the university to start a charity race between the athletes Steve Cram and Sebastian Coe, which re-enacted the famous race around Trinity College from the Oscar-winning film *Chariots of Fire*. Edward followed his tried-and-tested dating technique, inviting her to supper at Buckingham Palace. She also joined him at a Christmas Party there and was his guest for a weekend at Sandringham. Anwen is a bright girl who managed a 2.1 honours degree and was not afraid to give her point of view, especially if it involved deflating one of Edward's pompous opinions. Inevitably their friendship leaked to the Press, which did not please Edward one bit. Anwen retreated to her college room while porters kept away journalists. Her parents Barry, an insurance broker, and Valerie, sensibly kept quiet and Anwen has never uttered a word about Edward, which probably explains why they are still friends eight years later. In March 1993, just a few months before he met Sophie, he joined a gang of 12 celebrating Anwen's 26th birthday with a spaghetti dinner at an Italian restaurant in Chelsea. By this time Anwen was carving out a career in the City, rather like Georgia May. She sees Edward regularly in her capacity as part of his Special Projects Group, which plans fund-raising schemes for the Duke of Edinburgh's Award Scheme.

One common theme that runs puzzlingly through Prince Edward's list of girls is that the majority appeared to have other boyfriends at the time they went out with the Prince. Romy Adlington, Georgia May, Ulrika Jonsson, Anastasia Cook and Anwen were all said to have had real boyfriends while Edward was just a 'friend'. This was perhaps taken to an extreme when it was revealed that world champion showjumper Gail Greenough was actually engaged to video producer Steve Mahaney and, according to some sources, broke it off because she was so keen on Edward. That may or may not have been the case but, like Anwen, Gail has remained friends with Edward since she first met him at the *It's A Royal Knock-Out* event. As one observer commented, 'It was lucky she was there. He really needed a friend after that.' Gail won the world showjumping title in 1986 and was at the top of her sport, which really impressed Edward who has always been very keen on riding. She was first 'linked' with him after his romance with Georgia May fizzled out and she joined him on an official visit to Canada. She spent a weekend at a lakeside mansion in Ontario where he was staying and admitted, 'He's great company and a lovely man.' Being great company included, to the incredulity of watching photographers, unfastening the back of her dress at a ball in Toronto. She also joined him on a skiing holiday in Whistler, British Columbia. Gail, four years older than Edward and larger than life, was 'smuggled' into the Berkeley Square Ball, which was one of the liveliest summer social events in London during the 1980s. For a while they seemed keen on each other, but the Atlantic Ocean did not make the heart grow fonder when she returned to Canada. Funnily enough, Gail was even linked with the Prince after he had started going out with Sophie. She had flown into London for a six-week stay and confirmed she would be seeing Edward because 'he is a friend of mine'. By then, of course, Edward had eyes only for Sophie but no one knew that at the time.

Edward's position at the Really Useful Company put him in pole position for meeting attractive girls involved in the theatre. They flitted in and out of his life like butterflies. A single date, however, does not an engagement make and looking back it is absolutely ridiculous that Edward should have been 'married off' in the eyes of the world to any of his girlfriends before Sophie. Although he was and remains very fond of some of them, the fact is that they were not really serious enough to warrant speculation on engagements let alone marriage. It was only when Sophie emerged as the most important woman in his life that Edward's real attitude to marriage was revealed. As one Royal expert put it, 'It's not that he doesn't take marriage seriously. He takes it very seriously indeed, which is why he is so anxious not to make a mistake.' In these early carefree days in the theatre he was 'linked' with Marsha Bland, a vivacious actress who danced in Edward's favourite musical *Cats*, Andrew Lloyd Webber's secretary Jane Sann and Catherine Caldicott, who was personal assistant to the composer's former wife Sarah Brightman. There was very little in these supposed liaisons — Marsha, needless to say, was living with her boyfriend at the time.

Of more significance was the talented and successful musical star Ruthie Henshall whose career has been on the up and up since she first started a friendship with Edward when she was in *Cats*. Ruthie is a bundle of singing and dancing energy who, during the time she was close to Edward, gave him a much-needed injection of glamour. Her story reads like the plot of a Hollywood musical, a meteoric rise from a Clacton-on-Sea revue to headlining star of *Crazy For You* and *She Loves You*. In the best of showbiz traditions she was an understudy in the musical *Miss Saigon* who stepped in when one of the leading actresses was taken ill and was a huge hit. Throw in a dalliance with a Prince of the Realm and true love with actor John Gordon Sinclair and you can imagine Ruthie playing herself in a film biography. *The Prince and the Showgirl* would have been a good title if it had not already been used. As her career began to take off Ruthie, who had admitted to being desperate to be a star, became very defensive about her association with Edward. She moaned: 'I am Ruthie Henshall. I am not and do not want to be known as Ruthie Henshall, friend of Prince Edward.'

Their special relationship blossomed in 1990 when she trod the well-worn path to Buckingham Palace and Sandringham, and Edward was a regular visitor to her parents' home in the small village of Stutton, Suffolk. Edward was one of the guests who whooped it up at her 23rd birthday party at an Ipswich hotel. Edward was and remains a great admirer of Ruthie. In a bygone age he would have been a Stagedoor Johnny waiting to greet her after another barn-storming performance with a bouquet of roses and an enthusiastic 'Darling, you were wonderful'. Exactly how intimate their friendship was is a secret between them, but after *Cats* Ruthie moved on to a show called *Children of Eden* where she fell for fellow actor Adrian Beaumont who became her live-in lover at a flat in Peckham. By the end of 1992 that relationship was over and Edward was seen having dinner with Ruthie thereby fanning the flame of romantic gossip. Edward, however, was merely a good friend and cheering Ruthie up. In the months before he met Sophie she was a regular guest at Buckingham Palace, but dismissed any romantic notions. She declared: 'I go to Buckingham Palace when I visit Prince Edward because that is where he lives.'

The biggest break in Ruthie's career came in early 1993 when she was chosen to play the lead in the Broadway hit musical *Crazy For You* which was opening in the West End at, of all places, the Prince Edward Theatre. Edward was thrilled when Ruthie, whose talent he so much admired, won the part. He was her escort at a very public night out at the fashionable River Café in Fulham where they were joined by the show's director Mike Ockrent, choreographer Susan Stroman, writer Ken Ludwig and leading man Kirby Ward. Afterwards Ruthie said, 'We have a great time together and we have a mutual interest in the theatre.'

Applying the 'smuggling' criteria, this 'affair' seemed a little too public to be real. An example of the true nature of their friendship and of Edward's respect for Ruthie came when he missed Ruthie's opening night triumph in *Crazy For You*. It turned out to be the evening that Edward went out with Anwen Roberts and friends to celebrate her 26th birthday. Ruthie explained: 'We'd agreed there would be no way he'd come tonight. We don't want a circus.' It was Ruthie's big moment and Edward demonstrated commendable sensitivity by not stealing any of her limelight. One of the best compliments ever paid to Prince Edward came from Ruthie's mother Gloria who said, after her daughter had fallen in love with John Gordon Sinclair, 'Edward woke her up to the fact that nice men are much nicer to be with and I thank him for that.'

From Ruthie to Sophie is not the big leap it might

appear. Sophie's extrovert good-fun nature and her acting and dancing training are not a million miles away from Ruthie. Nor does it take too much imagination to picture Sophie hoofing enthusiastically in the chorus of a West End musical. Edward is intoxicated by theatre folk, their outgoing personalities and lack of inhibitions. They give him the confidence to be himself and relax. Whenever he is out with his theatrical friends the night is always alive with the sound of Edward's booming laughter. One of his fondest memories is of his informal 25th birthday party at a restaurant in Covent Garden. Three of the girls from *Cats* — Marsha Bland, Ria Jones and Ruthie Henshall — each sang him a love song. Marsha sang 'The Man That Got Away' from *A Star is Born*, Ria offered the Tim Rice song 'I Know Him So Well' and Ruthie rendered the classic Judy Garland song 'You Made Me Love You.' Edward Windsor loved every minute of it.

Ruthie and Edward are still good friends and she is now a good friend of Sophie's as well. They were all amused that the first time Edward and Sophie appeared in public together, Ruthie was there, too, and the photographers had eyes only for her and the Prince, thereby missing the best picture. When Sophie and Edward met, his romantic life was really in calm waters. It was as if he was asleep on a lilo in the middle of a still swimming-pool just waiting for someone to jump in and make waves. The Norwegian Love Boat was an attempt to whip up a few breakers, but it barely caused a ripple. He came back from cruising the fjords romantically becalmed. It would take a kiss from Sophie to waken this sleeping Prince.

12

Nearly Useful, Very Ardent

It is not easy for a member of the Royal Family to start work as a 'junior'. In a society where every door you could possibly want to open is immediately unlocked and pushed ajar by someone anxious to please, it would be simpler to start at the top. Edward did not want that soft option. He was determined to stand on his own two feet in the private sector, unfettered by Royal traditions but he was faced with a dilemma — how do you start on the factory floor when you are a Prince? He knew that he wanted to pursue a career in the world of theatre and entertainment, but he was a novice and needed to learn his trade just as a carpenter's apprentice would. It is important to understand the strength of character that Edward has shown in shaping his own destiny in order to obtain a clearer insight into the way his relationship with Sophie has developed. That relationship has matured at a pace set by Edward —

not by his family, not by Palace courtiers and most definitely not by the Press. Edward wants to be in control and, since he prised himself away from the Marines, he alone has made the important decisions in his life. That is why he was able to take a lowly paid job with Andrew Lloyd Webber's Really Useful Theatre Group with the full support of his mother and father. He was the first of the Queen's children to be an 'employee' and he would have to face up to a fair share of teasing as a result. However, being the target of sniping and innuendo has only ever toughened Edward's resolve.

Edward first came into contact with the celebrated composer when he decided to put on a show to celebrate the Queen's 60th birthday. His enthusiasm for new projects is one of his most endearing qualities and he immediately set about writing to the man at the top of his profession. Lloyd Webber and his most famous partner Tim Rice produced a mini-operetta entitled *Cricket*, which poked gentle fun at supporters of that most English of games. It was performed in front of the Queen, King Hussein of Jordan and other guests at Windsor Castle and featured the talented actor Ian Charleson, star of *Chariots of Fire*, who died tragically young from an Aids-related illness. In the run-up to this celebration Edward forged a friendship with Lloyd Webber's executive director Biddy Hayward who, realising the depth of Edward's desire for a career in the theatre, was largely responsible for brokering the deal that ended up with Edward starting work on 15 February, 1988 as a production assistant with Really Useful. Biddy was also unwittingly responsible for Edward being labelled as the tea-boy. In answer to a question of whether Edward would be brewing up she told a journalist,

'Everyone makes the tea. He will have to make the tea and answer the telephones like the rest of us. We all muck in and Edward is starting on the lowest rung.' That was all the encouragement the Press needed and poor Edward was lumbered as the 'Royal tea-boy'. At least he was not po-faced about it and took it the right way, rolling up for his first day at the aptly named Palace Theatre with a packet of PG Tips in his hand.

Edward revelled in his first taste of freedom in the real world as plain Edward Windsor. By no stretch of the imagination could he ever be said to lead a normal life — not too many office juniors go to work every day with a detective. Neither are many addressed as 'Sir' by senior staff outside the office. One observer said, 'He is surrounded by people who cannot forget he is the Queen's youngest son. It really is impossible trying to be an ordinary person and a Royal.' Simple things that the rest of us would take for granted were among Edward's greatest pleasures. He loved joining workmates for lunch in the small bistros and sandwich bars of Soho. He joined a gang of colleagues who were all taken out to lunch by Andrew Lloyd Webber at The Last Days of the Raj, the fashionable Indian restaurant where he would take Sophie at a later date. He enjoyed being able to walk amid the hustle and bustle of Soho with no one taking a blind bit of notice of a Prince of the Realm. It did not always work in his favour, however — like the time he was late for a meeting and found the street doors were locked. He tried the intercom but no one heard, so Prince Edward was left hanging around on the doorstep like an unwelcome carol singer.

If he could not be an actor himself then, in working in the theatre, he was tasting the next best thing. At a time when Sophie was enjoying rubbing shoulders with the media at Capital Radio, Edward was doing the same at Really Useful. There are an intriguing number of similarities in the way both their careers paths have unwound. Just as Edward needed to find a new direction and purpose in life after his exit from the Marines so Sophie took time off to travel to Crans-Montana and Australia before finding the career she enjoys as a publicity and media consultant. Both of them take their careers very seriously and they tackle everything with considerable enthusiasm, a shared characteristic that has helped to cement their relationship.

At this stage of his career on the 'bottom rung' Edward's ambition was to be a theatre producer. He saw himself as a Cameron Mackintosh or Florenz Ziegfeld figure producing the latest musical blockbusters like *Miss Saigon* and *Les Miserables* and winning glowing praise from respected columnists. Edward is ambitious but he also craves praise. That need to have someone say, 'Brilliant, Sir', or 'Well done!' was partly responsible for his disastrous brush with the Press at *It's a Royal Knock-Out*. For the moment his drive was firmly channelled in getting off the bottom rung at Really Useful. After spending a few months settling in, it became apparent to senior executives that Edward was a very good organiser.

Whatever other judgements are made about *It's a Royal Knock-Out*, Edward cannot be faulted on the brilliant organisation. It was his forte in his light entertainment ventures at Cambridge and he has always been to the fore in arranging family entertainments. In October 1988 he organised a spectacular 40th birthday party for Prince Charles in the Picture Gallery of Buckingham Palace. Phil Collins provided the cabaret and Barry Humphries, Elton

John, Billy Connolly and, of course, Andrew Lloyd Webber joined the guests. It was a great success. If Edward had been a film star he would have been Mickey Rooney forever 'putting on a show' while Judy Garland looked on adoringly.

Edward's basic job was gluing things together so that overseas productions of the Lloyd Webber hits went well. He became Overseas Co-ordinator and helped to get *Aspects of Love* ready for Broadway. He was involved with the French production of *Cats*, the Vienna version of *Phantom of the Opera* and the new-look London production of *Starlight Express*. The Broadway opening of *Aspects of Love* was to prove a watershed for the years of gossip and innuendo that Edward had suffered about his sexuality. It is easily forgotten that all the time Edward was working for Really Useful, he had another job, too. The Queen had insisted that he continue to pull his weight as a Royal and justify his £20,000 Civil List allowance. He tried to limit his Royal engagements to weekends, but this was not always possible and sometimes he would do three or four 'jobs' in a week. He would get home to Buckingham Palace no earlier than 7.00pm and get straight into a dinner suit to attend a function where he would be guest of honour. Edward was still only 24, but he was beginning to realise that there was too much conflict of interest in having two jobs and it would not be long before something would have to give.

In 1989, a year after he joined Really Useful, Edward spent three days in Moscow as a guest of the National Youth Theatre who were performing *Murder in the Cathedral* at the Moscow Arts Theatre. This was shortly after President Gorbachev had come to England and was seen as a further building of bridges. He visited Red Square and the Kremlin and saw the Bolshoi Ballet perform *Giselle*. Once again his unfortunate pompous streak surfaced when Edward was asked by a man from the Russian news service Tass, 'When you go home what will you tell your mother about Russia?' Edward replied, 'I hope you're not referring to Her Majesty The Queen.' If only Edward could get rid of this hint of arrogance, he might find the great British public far more forgiving. As it was, when he returned to England he walked into a row about the cost of sending him to Moscow — the newspapers estimated that the trip cost £100,000 and was a waste of taxpayers' money. Although the trip was sponsored, it further undermined Edward's position on the Civil List. Something would have to be done.

After two years at Really Useful, Edward's ambition began to get the better of him. There were some rumblings within the theatre division that they were no longer in the forefront of Andrew Lloyd Webber's thinking. However, there was also the realisation that he needed to earn real money because it now seemed a case of when, rather than if, the Civil List allowance dried up. Perhaps of even more importance at this stage was the deterioration in the professional relationship of Andrew Lloyd Webber and Biddy Hayward, who had started off as his secretary 17 years earlier, but had now outgrown her role as trusty lieutenant. What came next was in the nature of a military coup with one slight drawback — it turned out to be a humiliating failure.

The seeds of the 'mutiny' were sewn at the Scandic Crown Hotel near Victoria Station, just around the corner from Buckingham Palace. This meant that Edward could sneak out just before midnight and

The best
of friends.

Top: The picture that started it all. Sophie and Edward were instantly easy in each other's company. Ironically, they have never again been pictured so close.

Below: Sophie had to get used to the welcoming committee of paparazzi when she arrived for work at her Hammersmith offices.

Sophie leaves her company's Christmas party in December 1995 with boss Brian MacLaurin shortly after handing in her notice. At the time it looked as though Santa would be bringing news of her engagement – but in the event she had three more years to wait for that!

Talk of marriage reached fever pitch whenever Sophie and Edward attended a friend's wedding. In 1994 there were so many that Sophie and Edward were fast becoming the only unmarried couple they knew.

The wet look makes a splash, windsurfing off Cowes in 1994.

Top: Sophie has been having lessons to become a crack shot, but on her first visit to Sandringham in the New Year of 1994 she had to take the role of beater, disturbing the birds for the others to shoot.

Below: She has never lost touch with her friends despite the royal circles she mixes in. Here she joines pals on a weekend trip to Dartmouth in Devon.

Sophie's natural charm and down-to-earth personality have quickly made her a national favourite.

A princess in waiting – but not for much longer!

meet his six colleagues, including Biddy who later dismissed speculation that this was a meeting of clandestine conspirators and insisted it was just standard production business. The 'Magnificent Seven' ate a light supper and chatted until 2.00am when they emerged to be greeted by a posse of paparazzi who had received a tip-off. So much for secrecy. If it had been a real military coup there would have been seven more behind the bars of a jail before daybreak. Within two months all seven had left Andrew Lloyd Webber to set up a rival business. Biddy Hayward had been sacked at the beginning of June and the other six, including Edward, walked out the door three weeks later.

Prince Edward issued a statement from Buckingham Palace: 'I am particularly grateful to Andrew Lloyd Webber and the Really Useful Group for their support and encouragement over the last couple of years and especially for giving me the chance to work in the theatre professionally. I hope to use this experience to progress further into production and explore new areas.' Andrew Lloyd Webber was 'deeply offended' at the mutiny, although officially his spokesman said he was very relaxed about it all and wished everyone well. And so a company called Theatre Division was formed, with Edward Windsor as technical director. Lloyd Webber would have been forgiven for laughing his socks off as the company went down the toilet within a year.

In retrospect Edward must have been mad to leave Lloyd Webber, as he was doing well there. The company was the most successful of its kind in the country. He was protected from the glare of outside criticism by the corporate umbrella and by the genius of a man with a theatrical Midas touch. However,

Biddy Hayward was his friend and it was through her support and encouragement that he had a start in a career he loved. Edward does not let go a friend's hand when they are dangling over the side of a cliff. There was never any question of him not joining the lady who was in effect his theatrical mentor.

The Magnificent Seven did not know it at the time, but they were embarking on their adventure at a time when the West End was about to go through a relatively lean period. Everyone would soon be feeling the pinch and the Gulf War would keep many American tourists at home. In the end, Theatre Division lasted a year and put on two productions in the West End. The first featured the actress Nicola Pagett in a comedy called *The Rehearsal* by the post-war French dramatist Jean Anouilh. It opened at the Almeida Theatre in North London and transferred to the Garrick Theatre in the West End. Any West End theatre does not come cheap so, although the play was nominated for a prestigious Olivier award, it was not the roaring commercial success that the company needed to work up a head of steam. While *The Rehearsal* gasped for commercial breath they put *Same Old Moon* by Irish playwright Geraldine Aron into production. It had been personally recommended to Biddy Hayward by Prince Edward, but despite everyone's best efforts it struggled for a foothold at a difficult time. It opened at The Globe and just six weeks later the curtain came down for the final time. Exciting plans to stage a musical revival of *Billy* were shelved and on 12 July, 1991 Theatre Division collapsed with debts of £600,000. Andrew Lloyd Webber's response to the news that the venture had failed was a masterful one. He said: 'I wish Biddy could have told me because, perhaps, I could have whacked some money in.' As a delicious extra touch of irony, that same month he 'whacked in' £100,000 to help save The Almeida where Theatre Division had staged their very first production.

Is someone somewhere sticking pins into a voodoo doll of Prince Edward? He does not exactly have a Midas touch — the Marines, *It's a Royal Knock-Out* and now Theatre Division would not light up anyone's CV. Edward was 27, unemployed with a recently increased Civil List allowance of £100,000 per year. The natives in the Press were growing restless at what was perceived as an exorbitant sum for the seventh in line to the throne. Edward was under a lot of pressure to fulfil both private and public roles. The only way was up.

He did not give up or even spend time licking wounds. Instead, within six months the foundation for his future career was in place. It was to be television. Up until this time theatre had been Edward's great love and television was something you watched if there was nothing better to do. The workings of television production were completely foreign to Edward, but he plunged himself into a new venture with typical enthusiasm. He had to do something because the formation of Ardent Productions — managing director Edward Windsor — coincided with the loss of his Civil List allowance. It is not every day that £100,000 disappears from one's bank account, even if your mother is happy to finance official expenditure. To suggest that Edward was in any way strapped for cash is slightly ludicrous. When he founded Ardent he managed to put up £205,000 of his own money, making him by far the majority shareholder. In addition nearly £750,000 was invested by anonymous backers, although most shrewd observers believe Edward's angel to be the Sultan of Brunei, one of the richest men in the world. Edward became quite friendly with the Sultan's son on a visit to Brunei in 1992. They played a lot of golf together, which is not Edward's best sport. He is an appalling hacker but, as he so often is away from public scrutiny, the Prince was the life and soul of the fairways. On that trip Edward had the difficult choice of finding a present for the Sultan, a man who could literally buy anything his heart desired. In the end Edward gave him a signed original water colour by Prince Charles. The Sultan was delighted with the personal touch and responded warmly and encouragingly to Edward's new business venture.

Edward is never going to be a great media tycoon. He is not a flamboyant Lew Grade figure forever sporting a cigar as big as a flagpole. Nor will he ever be a hard-nosed mogul like Rupert Murdoch. Edward has ideas, organisational ability and enormous enthusiasm. He does not have the knack of making money as Ardent's balance sheets have shown, although in the New Year of 1997 his luck began to take a decisive turn for the better. It needed to — in only its first year of operation Ardent went £450,000 into the red. This was even more disappointing because a prestigious documentary involving Edward interviewing Nelson Mandela fell by the wayside. When he formed Ardent Edward stridently affirmed: 'Making a Royal programme would give the wrong impression, I don't want to trade on that association any more than I intend trading on my title.' That is a very laudable intention, but there is nothing like a loss of close on half a million smackers for bringing someone to their senses.

Edward's first idea was a documentary on real

tennis, which would probably have been topped in the ratings by the test card. We shall never know whether Channel 4 would have been as keen to commission this programme if Prince Edward had not been the presenter. If Edward had not developed a passion for the game at Cambridge and become a 'realer' he might never have met Sophie. He took up the game because rugby was proving to be a health hazard. He explained: 'I'd become such a target on the rugby field that I seemed to spend most of my time injured and so I wanted to play a more civilised, gentlemanly game. I'd always had a problem with lawn tennis because the net was too high and the court too small but with real tennis I could belt the ball back as hard as possible and it would still come back into court off the high back wall — perfect for a slogger like me.'

Much more ambitious was Ardent's first venture into drama. The satirical soap *Annie's Bar* failed to capture the public imagination, although it was competent. It was not re-commissioned by Channel 4. Edward did better with his own starring performance in front of the camera for his documentary on Edward VIII. It was called *Edward on Edward* and the post-Sophie Prince was a poised and relaxed presenter. Edward also revealed a charisma previously hidden from the world. He is never going to be a hunk, but the thirty-something Prince showed every indication of using his prestige and celebrity to better effect than he had done in his troubled twenties. It did not, however, take Edward very long to eat his brave words and make a Royal programme, although he should not be too hard on himself for cashing in on his obvious connections. *Edward on Edward* was a good idea and, considering the debate over the title of HRH for Diana and Fergie, seemed strangely topical as it explored the controversy of not giving the HRH title to the Duchess of Windsor. He was probably too soft on his great-uncle.

The fact of life for an independent television production company is that the majority of time and energy is spent on developing an idea. You have to think of a good theme, then talk about it a great deal and then try to sell it. Edward, because of who he is, has a head start in getting to talk to the right people but his ideas, like everyone's, rise or fall on their own merit. If the idea is no good then no one will buy it — not even if it is pitched by the Queen's son. For an independent production company, it is all about building contacts and finding out what makes a commissioning editor tick. Like his competitors Edward went off to the Cannes Television Festival to try to 'schmooze' potential clients. In keeping with his intention of being an ordinary bloke he flew economy and avoided the five-star hotels.

The breakthrough for Ardent and Edward came in the USA. The giant CBS network was impressed with his *Edward on Edward* series and, in particular, with his style of presenting. They signed up Ardent to make eight programmes in a deal worth an estimated £2 million. This will effectively wipe out the company's three-year loss of some £1 million and set them on a successful path. Edward could be forgiven for shouting his success from the rooftops, but the new Prince prefers to take things in his sober stride. It is a triumph for hard work. He is at his desk at 8.30am trying to find the right formula to thrust his company into a higher echelon of independent producers. Now he has succeeded. The small print of the deal is that Edward will present the programmes himself. This is no great hardship after his accomplished performance on *Edward on Edward*. It may well be that his future lies in this direction. Producing and presenting may be a combination that, given his track record, would be the best of both worlds. Presenting is, after all, a form of acting.

13

Signs and Whispers

If £100 was offered to charity for every rumour that a public figure was gay, there would be no need for good causes to petition the National Lottery for funds. Newspaper offices are awash with gossip about pop stars, film stars, politicians and members of the Royal Family being secret homosexuals. Some of the rumours turn out to be true in the saddest of circumstances, as in the Aids-related deaths of Rock Hudson and Freddie Mercury. Others are discovered to be true because those involved no longer wish to keep their sexuality hidden, as in the cases of Elton John, Michael Barrymore and George Michael. Some remain forever hidden from the gaze of the general public. Prince Edward is a special case. The 'is he or isn't he?' gay debate has been fully aired in the media, even though there has never been one shred of acceptable evidence offered as proof that he is. No rent boy or jilted male lover has ever appeared in the pages of the Sunday newspapers and told of a torrid affair with the Queen's youngest son. The *News of the World* did publish some dubious second-hand claims in 1986, but these were not considered worthy of comment. It is rough justice for Edward, although to some extent the free-for-all debate about his sexuality is his own fault. Until Sophie arrived in his life the question remained — is Edward an eligible bachelor or just a confirmed one? The gossip has added an extra dimension to Edward's blossoming relationship with Sophie. Royal commentators have suggested that marriage and a family will put the whisperers firmly in their place. If he doesn't marry Sophie, he lays himself open to the 'well, he was gay all along' type of remark.

It really does not take very much for a rumour to gain some momentum. The jump from being labelled a bit of a 'mummy's boy' to Palace Queen is a small one. It is a well-worn joke that there is more than one Queen at Buckingham Palace because the place is full of homosexual servants. At Cambridge there was allegedly a compromising photograph of Edward in circulation, but this has never surfaced. When he left the Marines at the same time as a male chum it was hinted that Edward was not manly enough for this particular occupation. Then he joined a theatrical world where he was surrounded by luvvies and camp followers who gave him the nicknames 'Dockland Doris' and 'Barbara' Windsor, which provided more ammunition to the 'wink-wink, nudge-nudge' brigade. The entire issue really does beg the question, 'Is that all there is to it?' The gossip, such as it was, would probably have been confined to Chelsea dinner parties and Fleet Street bar-stools if Edward had not taken the highly risky step of declaring to the world in 1990: 'I'm not gay.' Up until then the idea that he might have been would never have crossed the minds of the great majority of people.

The story unfolded in New York when Edward flew there for the première of the Lloyd Webber musical *Aspects of Love* starring the handsome and popular Michael Ball. Although the singer had a girlfriend, the former *Ready, Steady, Go* presenter Cathy McGowan, she was nearly 20 years older than him. Ball was also remembered as being the young man who was once covered in gold paint and leapt from a box as a surprise birthday present for Elton John's manager John Reid. It had been hinted in the papers that a touching friendship had developed between Michael and Edward, a suggestion that thoroughly upset Edward.

The first night of *Aspects of Love* was a great success and everyone was in high spirits at the party afterwards, which was held in the Rockefeller Center. Edward was at a table that included Peter Brown, former partner and best friend of Brian Epstein in the days of The Beatles and now a New York-based business consultant whose clients include The Really Useful Group. Peter, who is straightforward and honest about his own homosexuality, recalls: 'A journalist who was not on the list of invited guests came up and asked a question about the show. Edward gave a nice reply. I think the journalist must have thought "This is easy", because a short while later he approached Edward again. He asked him directly 'Are you gay?' I think Edward was rather taken aback. You have to realise that Edward is very, very polite in any social situation and would never rudely ignore an approach.'

Throughout his life Edward has been plagued by his mouth moving ahead of his brain — Prince Philip, the world champion, calls it 'Dentopedology', the art of putting one's foot in one's mouth — and here was another occasion. Instead of ignoring the intrusion he exploded in anger: 'It's just outrageous to suggest this sort of thing. It's so unfair to me and my family. How would you feel if someone said you were gay? The rumours are preposterous. I am not gay, but what can I do about it? Why do certain people try to make more of things? I can only repeat — it's very unfair. The Press has to be a lot more responsible. I wish I could be left to enjoy the theatre. I love it.'

In hindsight, it is easy to say that Edward should have sent the reporter packing with a flea in his ear, but he is not that sort of man. Just as he had given the newspapers their story during *It's A Royal Knock-Out* he did so again on what should have been just another opening night on Broadway. If he had ignored this particularly brazen reporter there would have been no story. Instead next day the *Daily Mirror* had a great scoop: 'QUEEN'S SON POURS HIS HEART OUT TO THE *MIRROR* - I'M NOT GAY!' Edward may have thought he was setting the record straight, but in effect all he did was start the record. In a million pubs that day people would say over their pints, 'Did you read in the paper about Prince Edward being gay?' Mud sticks.

The New York incident was just the excuse the papers needed to discuss Edward's sexuality in a series of follow-ups. The *Daily Mirror* wrote: 'Prince Edward's astonishing decision to tell the world "I'm not gay" means cruel whispers about his private life can be openly discussed for the first time.' Edward was mortified that he had been the source of this free-for-all, although to suggest that his off-the-cuff remarks were in any way a public statement would be stretching the point.

The 'evidence' was thoroughly explored in the Press — his latest nickname among his workmates at the Really Useful Group was 'Mavis'; he was sent to Gordonstoun by his father to 'make a man of him'; he was a 'wimp' on the rugby field; he wore a medieval costume with a feathered hat on *It's A Royal Knock-Out*; he was called the Apple-Juice kid by fellow recruits in the Marines; he wears Elton-John-style blousy blue silk jackets with carefully cut jeans; he's 26 and he is not married. And there, ladies and gentlemen of the jury, the prosecution rests.

The defence presented a list of people anxious to support the view of a heterosexual prince. His former girlfriend and lover Romy Adlington was smartly out of the blocks declaring: 'He's a real man. I was horrified to hear the rumours. There's no question of the Prince being homosexual. Nothing is further from the truth. He's heterosexual and very manly.' Romy's mother Anne Adlington endorsed her daughter's opinion by saying: 'He is definitely not gay. I think women can tell.' Ruthie Henshall's father David was more forceful and declared: 'It's contemptible. The attack on the guy is totally out of order.' Royal biographer Brian Hoey said: 'I have been in his company at various gatherings and I would say he definitely has an eye for the girls.'

And that is just about all one can say on the matter. In the absence of any real facts the entire story was fed and nurtured with a series of negatives, a classic newspaper ploy that Edward had initiated by his own 'I'm not gay' outburst. The clumsiest of his remarks in retrospect was, 'How would you like it if someone called *you* gay?' which is unlikely to be adopted as a slogan by homosexual pressure groups.

Edward, more sensibly, kept his mouth firmly shut on the matter, vowing in private not to be so hot-headed in future. In the absence of any real evidence it was impossible to sustain the story although Royal expert Margaret Holder observed, 'It had reached the point where Edward was being asked impertinent questions and subjected to gossip and he had decided he'd had enough. But I think speaking out is a mistake he might regret.'

Every so often over the next couple of years the story resurfaced. The London-based columnist Taki described Edward on American television as being 'very gay'. Ulrika Jonsson, more and more in the news, declared: 'No way is he gay. I know that for a fact. I'm not saying how I know, but he certainly finds women attractive.'

One thing that Edward has never done amid all the gossip and innuendo is sever ties with friends who are gay. It is really part and parcel of being in the theatrical world and in New York, where he is a frequent dinner guest of his friend Peter Brown, he has found it easier to mix socially with a wide variety of people. Peter's own view of Edward rests as the most understanding insight into the man and the whole gay question: 'As a *heterosexual* man Edward is very comfortable with gay people. That is only possible because he is so very secure with his own personality and his own sexuality.'

The closest that anyone has come to resurrecting the rumours about him was in the newspaper reports about his close friend Dieter Abt who was accused and subsequently cleared of a multi-million pound fraud. Dieter, handsome, flamboyant and single had been charged after his catering company, which held three Royal Warrants, crashed with massive debts. He had become friends with Edward because of their mutual interest in the National Youth Theatre. The unspoken implication was that Edward must be gay because he has a friend who is so flamboyant. Dieter, we learnt, held lavish celebrity-laden parties at his million-pound home in St John's Wood, London. On one occasion he threw a champagne and lobster party especially to cheer up Edward after the Prince had phoned to say he was bored. Michael Caine, Marie Helvin, Michael Winner and Joan Collins were among those rubbing shoulders with the Prince who had a great time.

Edward, happy and relaxed, posed for a picture with Dieter, something the secretive Prince very rarely does. It was Dieter who was credited with giving Edward the nickname 'Dockland Doris' and he also gave Edward a solid silver miniature of an actor's table. After he was found not guilty, Dieter returned to Switzerland to live and his friendship with Edward faltered. He said: 'If I had wanted to get in touch I could have done. I just didn't want to embarrass anybody.'

The arrival in his life of Sophie Rhys-Jones has effectively silenced the whispers about Edward's sexuality. Although he has had quite a few girlfriends and was certainly no virgin where women are concerned the suspicion was that, until Sophie, members of the opposite sex were more friends than lovers.

Women who meet the Prince and enjoy his company certainly seem to discount any theories that he might be gay. Jayne Fincher, who has taken many official photographs of the Prince and has been his guest at the ballet, observed: 'He gets on very well with women and is easy-going in their company. He is like his brother Charles in that respect. You know almost immediately when you speak to someone who's gay. You recognise it as a woman. I've never had that feeling about Prince Edward.'

So what does Sophie herself make of the rumours that Edward is gay? She is incandescent with rage at the mere suggestion. It is clearly the most powerful argument against the whispers that plague her Prince. When her friend and colleague Nick Skeens asked her how Edward reacted to the accusations that he was gay, Sophie quickly became angry and said, 'It doesn't bother him too much but it bothers me.' Nick recalls: 'Sophie went into an explanation of how, when Edward was in the theatre, there were a couple of people who claimed they had slept with him. She felt it was in the nature of some theatre people, because it's such a gay community, to claim they had slept with him. But she said to me very clearly, "I CAN ABSOLUTELY ASSURE YOU FROM MY EXPERIENCE THAT THAT MAN IS NOT GAY."'

Part Three

14

When Sophie Met Edward

When Sophie met Edward for the first time she took her top off. Not just once but many times. It was all in the line of duty, of course, and she was wearing a white 'body' underneath, but it's quite a good way to make an impression and, although he maintained a traditionally regal sang-froid, there is no doubt that Edward noticed that Sophie was a very fit girl.

Their meeting came about because of a completely unforeseen set of circumstances. It should not have been Sophie at that particular Royal photocall flinging T-shirts on and off with good-natured abandon but sports presenter Sue Barker. The event was the brainchild of Sophie's boss Brian MacLaurin and, like most Royal engagements, it was all for charity. Brian had been asked by the Radio Authorities chairman Peter Baldwin to drum up some interest in a charity project called the Prince Edward Summer Challenge, which was linked to the Duke of Edinburgh's Award Scheme. Edward had put his name to the idea, which encouraged people to find sponsors for a particular challenge, the more daring the better. Each challenge would be within a commercial radio station's area and that station would give the entire event a great plug to drive as much money as possible into the appeal. The problem was that Edward is not the most charismatic figurehead as far as the general public is concerned — he has never courted that image — and the idea was not taking off at all. Enter Mr MacLaurin.

Brian said he would try to raise the profile of the Challenge and was phoned by the Prince's private secretary Sean O'Dwyer and asked to pop over to the Palace the following morning for breakfast to discuss his ideas with Edward. Over coffee and croissants Brian suggested that Edward had to try a challenge for himself. He argued that there was no point in just getting other people to do it. He had to do it as well. Brian promised to place a copy-cleared article in a national newspaper if Edward agreed to a challenge. What really impressed Edward were the magic words 'copy-cleared', which meant he would have final approval on what appeared in a newspaper. That was unheard of as far as he was concerned and he bit Brian's arm off in his enthusiasm to get involved.

Edward's challenge was to play real tennis. He could have streaked at Lords or skied down the Matterhorn naked with a rose between his teeth. But he decided to go on to the real tennis court at London's exclusive Queen's Club in West Kensington and play for as long as possible. The *Daily Mail* dutifully carried an uninspiring double-page spread on what he was going to do and what charities would benefit. Edward's 'copy-cleared' quote was: 'I think I'm completely mad, it's a heck of a long time but I'm hoping to have some fun.' Brian asked Sue Barker to get involved to spice up the photographs at the press-call to promote Edward's challenge. Sue was at last shaking off the shackles of once being a friend of Cliff Richard and had begun to carve out a career as a sports presenter with Sky, on her way to bigger and better things with the BBC. She was also the only half-decent, attractive tennis player Britain has produced in the last 20 years, so she was considered ideal to provide Edward with a touch of glamour. The cunning idea was that Sue would wear a series of sweat-shirts, each with a different commercial radio station's logo on the front — for instance, she would wear a Radio Clyde shirt and pose next to Prince Edward and that story would appear in the Glasgow papers. She would then change to a different station's logo so that another paper could be targeted. And so on.

Everything was arranged for the photocall and, at this stage, Sophie had nothing to do with it. As far as she was concerned it was just going to be an ordinary day at the office in Berghem Mews, Hammersmith. But fate took a hand when brusque Australian Dave Hill, the then Head of Sport at Sky Television, telephoned Brian MacLaurin and told him, 'Brian, under no circumstances am I going to have Sue Barker branded with anything other than Sky. There's no way. She's a Sky presenter.' 'Oh,' said Brian. 'You can't do it,' said Mr Hill and put the phone down. So with one hour to go before the photocall at Queen's Club, Brian was faced with the arrival of Prince Edward, his private secretary, a photographer, a bunch of T-shirts and nobody to wear them. Brian toyed briefly with the idea of asking Edward to model the shirts himself. Then he gazed around his office until he settled on Sophie working on a Press release. 'Sophie,' he purred in his smoothest Glaswegian, 'fancy popping down to Queen's Club with me?'

Sophie's flat in Vereker Road was just around the corner from Queen's, where every June the top tennis players warm up for Wimbledon in the Stella Artois tournament. It's a snooty place, as demonstrated by the rows the club have had with the great John McEnroe. On the way there Sophie was able to dive in to her flat, slip on a leotard and touch up her make-up before meeting Edward. Sophie does not really suffer from nerves or you would never know it if she did. She literally bounced into Queen's ready to get on with her job. That is all this first meeting was — a job, not a date.

When Prince Edward arrived, Brian MacLaurin went over to him in the office where everything was being organised and said, 'Excuse me, Sir, we have a problem. Sue Barker can no longer do the photocall, but I have brought one of my staff. Would you mind posing for pictures with her?' Edward craned his neck round the door to sneak a look at Sophie. He liked what he saw. Her hair was blonde from the summer sun and she was smiling and chatting to the photographer. 'Delighted,' said Edward, 'it's not a problem.' One of the reasons that Sophie proved such a perfect picture partner for Edward was her stature. She shares her height with the Queen, Queen Mother and Princess Margaret who often wear high heels and big hats to create the illusion of presence when in fact they are quite petite. Edward, a slim 5ft 9ins, would not need to stand on a box to be photographed next to Sophie who measures an optimistic 5ft 4ins in her stockinged feet.

For the next two hours Sophie went on the real tennis court and swapped sweatshirts and leaned on his shoulder in a refreshingly natural manner. No wonder the photographs from that session have been so widely used. Edward is grinning from ear to ear dressed in his neatly pressed white tennis shirt and shorts — nothing Agassi-like about him. One of the great ironies about the Royal Family is that the closer they get to someone the further they stand away from them. In all subsequent photos Sophie always seems to be a good three steps behind Edward. The only picture the newspapers now use from the day they met is the one of Sophie wearing a TalkBack Radio sweatshirt because they went out of business and there's no copyright on that one. Strangely enough Royal author Andrew Morton secured one of the pictures from the session and sold it when he broke the original story of Sophie and Edward's romance to the papers. From the beginning Morton has had chapter and verse from some 'Deep Throat' on this relationship.

Edward did not get Sophie's phone number at this first meeting. Princes in general do not need to do that. They can get a flunky to do their dirty work. Afterwards Sophie was bubbling over with the excitement of it all. She returned to the office in high spirits and could not wait to see if the pictures made the papers. Brian MacLaurin, shrewdly realising she had been a hit, decided there and then that she should be his assistant on this account. Sophie was delighted, although she never gave any indication even at this early stage that she thought Edward was a hunk or that she fancied him in any way. Nobody at the photocall noticed any electricity between the two. There was never any question of Edward getting in touch immediately to suggest a trip to the pictures. At this stage their relationship was strictly business and Edward is very professional where work is involved. Sophie joined her boss for meetings at Buckingham Palace and helped Brian to get the publicity everyone wanted for the Challenge — incredibly, the real tennis marathon raised a handsome £29,000 for charity. She never discussed the Prince with the girls in the office, but she told her close friends that he seemed like a 'nice guy' and was always very charming to her. Her presence certainly guaranteed Edward's interest in the project and helped to smooth things along.

On the day of the Challenge, 13 September, 1993, several photographers turned up hoping to get a shot of Edward with the girl they thought was his girlfriend, the stage actress Ruthie Henshall. They had no idea that Edward and Ruthie had already split up. Sophie's favourite photographer Andrew Murray remembers that they all took pictures of Ruthie without realising that they should have been taking pictures of Sophie. He groans now when he remembers the picture that got away. 'Sophie actually said during the day that if I wanted a picture I would have to wait until 8 o'clock because the game was going on all day. I thought "No" so I left at 4 o'clock. Later on, I was kicking myself. Ruthie had just turned up to the real tennis as a friend. She and Sophie were very friendly. During the day I was speaking to Sophie and she was talking about Edward this and Edward that and that the Prince had been talking a lot about this game. I thought "that's a bit friendly" but I didn't click. A bit stupid, really. I should have put two and two together.'

Sophie and Andrew Murray had first met several years before when Sophie was at Capital Radio. Andrew had recently arrived in Britain and approached the station to do photographic work for their PR department. He spoke to Sophie who told him they paid £100 an hour and she would give him a call. He never heard from her. They didn't meet up again until the real tennis match. 'We got on really well. We laughed about the £100 an hour and we sort of clicked. She has been to

Australia and skied over there. She calls a spade a spade and I think that's great.' Andrew was not the only one who failed to notice any chemistry between Sophie and Edward. Actor Robert Powell's wife Babs, the former Pan's People dancer, was also there and later told friends she did not see any sparks fly at all. Sophie's old Capital Radio colleague Doctor Fox was also taking part and played against Edward. He was too busy trying to master the game to notice anything. He was impressed with Edward who he says seemed an exceedingly nice bloke. He observed: 'The Royals are brilliantly brought up as social communicators and they are good at meeting you and within four minutes making you feel you have had a nice conversation with them. Then they go off to the next guy they have to meet and do the same thing. My impression was he was as down to earth as a Prince of the Realm could be.'

A couple of months after their first meeting, towards the end of September, it seemed as if nothing was ever going to light a fire under Edward. He was paying the young PR lady a great deal of attention, but it did not appear that things were going to go any further. He was almost certainly waiting until the official business of the Real Tennis challenge had been completed. And then he telephoned Sophie at home out of the blue. She had given him her private phone number in case there were any problems with the Challenge and Brian MacLaurin could not be reached. You can imagine Sophie's excitement at picking up the phone and hearing Prince Edward's voice on the line. They chatted about the Challenge before Edward suggested she might like to join him for a game of real tennis and perhaps a bite of supper afterwards at the Palace. How much better that sounds than a game of snooker and a Big Mac — what girl could resist?

Real tennis has always had very strong Royal connections. In fact, in this context real does not mean 'genuine', but is the old French word for royal. The Australians call it royal tennis. It is probably only played by a couple of hundred people in this country. There are two reasons for the game languishing as a minority sport. First, very few of the specialist and expensive courts needed still exist — you cannot play five-a-side football on them so they have no other use other than for real tennis. The second reason is that you need to be a brain surgeon to understand the rules. The game is played on a specifically designed, enclosed court and bears a stronger resemblance to squash than lawn tennis as we know it today. Real tennis has a language all its own with a set of French terms like dedans, bisque, grille and tambour, which sound more like items from a bistro menu than a sporting encounter. Sophie could play a passable game of tennis, which would be a help, but her knowledge of the 'real' variety was limited to what she had picked up helping with the Challenge. The crucial part of the game was something called the 'chase', which was quite apt under the circumstances of a first date.

The evening itself whizzed by as first dates often do. Being a sporty girl Sophie was never one to go in much for dresses, so after a leisurely soak in the bathtub she settled on a smart woollen jacket and trousers for the evening and walked the short distance to Queen's Club. Sophie always presents a calm exterior, but who could blame her if she was bubbling with excitement inside. It's not every day a girl from Brenchley goes on a date with a prince. You shall go to the ball, Cinders. The irony was that having carefully got ready for the date, as any woman would have, Sophie would spend the first part of the evening rushing round a real tennis court like a demented bluebottle. As it happened, although Edward takes his sport very seriously, he was happy to just knock a few balls about trying to explain a little about the game to Sophie. It was more of an ice-breaker than a serious coaching lesson.

They were able to relax immediately in each other's company and the Prince told Sophie to call him Edward and not Sir. Sophie has the precious gift of making men feel totally at ease. She is good fun, but just as importantly she is a good listener. She also played a trump card at this early stage of their relationship by suggesting that she should take some proper lessons so that she could give the Prince a 'real game'. Edward beamed — his natural shyness melting in Sophie's smile. As a result, one of the first presents he gave her was her own real tennis racket.

They could have talked for hours by the courtside but supper at the Palace beckoned and Sophie was soon speeding through the gates of Buckingham Palace. Was this really happening to the former Brenchley waitress? On the occasions when a girl was brought back to the Palace, supper invariably followed a routine. It was prepared for him in advance in his private second-floor suite by his valet Brian and laid out as a buffet on a small card table covered with a linen cloth so that the Prince and his friend could help themselves. A bottle of Edward's favourite German white wine would be chilling in a cooler. There would also be plenty of Malvern water in the fridge. Best of all the couple were left alone — the valet and the detective were given the rest of the night off — so it was very cosy and very intimate.

And it was as if they had known each other for years. They had so much in common. When Edward's friend Peter Brown subsequently had dinner with them he was struck with the way they shared a similar sense of humour. Common ground was easily found through their mutual love of the theatre and they laughed at each other's favourite stories. They talked of the theatre and their stumbling attempts at acting at school. Edward told Sophie that his first starring role was as Mole in his prep school's production of *Toad of Toad Hall*. He told her he had never forgotten the first lines he ever spoke on stage and no, they weren't 'To be or not to be'. Rather, they were 'Scrape and scratch and scrabble and scrooge'. Sophie laughed enthusiastically as Edward remembered how he had to speak those unforgettable words while lurking beneath a trap-door with a completely empty stage above. 'Then, suddenly out I popped right there in the middle of the stage.' The Queen, who was in the audience, had loved it.

Sophie told Edward about Dulwich College Preparatory School and the local amateur dramatics in Brenchley. She remembered her first part playing the cockerel and treated him to her impression of a sleepy rooster awakening. And they swapped anecdotes about celebrities. Edward laughed uproariously at her Gene Pitney story, his familiar laughter ringing out and disturbing the quiet calm of the Palace corridors.

They talked and talked and found that they shared so many likes and dislikes. Edward was thrilled that, after his youthful dalliances with Sloaney models and theatrical ladies, he had found a down-to-earth girl who seemed to like the things he liked. It's not that easy for a prince to meet a girl like this. In fact, it is pretty impossible. It was purely by chance that a work opportunity had allowed him to break the ice with a girl without feeling too awkward about things. If Edward had made a list of the things they both enjoyed at the end of the evening, he could have included the theatre, cinema, skiing, sailing, swimming and walking in wellington boots. He wasn't too sure about drinking, but perhaps he could learn to like it as much as Sophie.

Edward gets up bright and early in the morning, so doesn't like to go to bed too late especially during the week. His valet brings him a cup of tea and a biscuit at 6.00am, so as the antique carriage clock in his sitting-room struck midnight the evening drew to a close. Edward insisted that his chauffeur take Sophie home and escorted her down to the waiting green Rover 8201, which would become a regular sight from now on purring along Vereker Road, West Kensington. They agreed that Edward would call to arrange a second date, perhaps to the theatre. Edward kissed her softly on the cheek before waving her off into the night. It had been wonderful.

15

Meeting Mother

Although it was the last thing on her mind after that glorious first date, it wasn't long before one of Sophie's friends asked a question that had her reaching for a medicinal brandy: 'When do you think he'll introduce you to his mother?' Sophie had never had a problem with mothers before. In fact, mothers in general doted on her 'girl next door' personality. She was pink and scrubbed as a child and she is pink and scrubbed as an adult. And Mums love that. The only problem was that Edward's mother was HM The Queen.

Sophie would have to practise her curtsy in case she received an invitation. It is easy for men who just have to incline their head and that counts as a bow. But a curtsy is very important in Royal circles — even Princess Anne still curtsies to the Queen in private. Although Sophie had a job involving meeting the public and also was well accomplished on the Fulham social circuit, having tea with the sovereign would be a mighty jump in class. Fortunately her flat mate Ulli had some minor aristocratic connections — she is related to a former German ambassador to the court of St James's — and is well versed in the silver cutlery stakes.

For the moment, however, Sophie was able to put the spectre of the sovereign to the back of her mind while she was swept along in the delight of a blossoming romance. Edward had often been 'in lust' before, but this was different. He found himself falling headlong in love with Sophie and behaved like a big kid going on a first date to the church disco. Edward was on the phone to her all the time, two or three times a day at the office and then again at night. On one occasion at work publicity manager Neil Crespin answered the phone and asked who was calling. 'Edward,' came the reply. 'Hello, Sir,' said Neil, instantly recognising the Royal voice. 'Oh, so you spotted the *nom de plume*,' said a disappointed Prince. 'Well, it was easy,' confided Neil, 'it *is* your name.' From then on Edward would always leave the name Richard or Gus when he called. He had never been a great one for nicknames ever since he was called 'Jaws' at school because of the heavy metal braces he wore on his teeth. For his part he was happy to call his new girlfriend 'Soph'. It was comfortable.

Their mutual affection was developing. A close friend of Sophie's observed: 'Sophie is good fun, a laugh, attractive and the sort of girl that most men would enjoy chatting with into the night. Edward is serious, quiet and, as is probably the case with most Royals, somewhat arrogant and overbearing. You wouldn't have thought they were at all suited. But when Edward is with Sophie, he becomes good fun, too. It's extraordinary the effect she has on him.'

The thing that Sophie found most difficult to get

used to when she went on dates with Edward was that there were always three of them — Edward, Sophie and Edward's detective Steve. For the Prince having a member of the Royal Family Protection Squad along was like putting on a tie in the morning. He was so used to it. Sophie found it more difficult. If Edward was driving himself, his detective was obliged to sit in the front passenger seat. Sophie would have to sit in the back and try to stretch forward to chat with him, which wasn't all that easy when you are somewhat diminutive. In the early days they would continue to play real tennis. Edward introduced her to Hampton Court where many of his friends played, including his coach Lesley Ronaldson who was also a real tennis champion. Robert Powell's wife Babs and Chris Tarrant's wife Ingrid invited Sophie to join them for their weekly girls' game, which was a relief to Sophie who was such a novice at the sport. They also went to the theatre and to the cinema, although these outings were rather fraught because Edward was so wary about being photographed with an attractive blonde girl on his arm. He also did not want the paparazzi waiting when he left the cinema or theatre. He was so determined to keep Sophie a secret that she had to stumble to her seat in the dark after the lights had gone down. Even though he no longer worked for the Really Useful group, Edward maintained strong ties with the company. If he wanted to go to see one of Andrew Lloyd Webber's shows he could be guaranteed discretion. They went to see *Phantom of the Opera* together and loved it, even though they had both already seen it more than once.

One of Edward's little weaknesses is curry, which is unusual for a member of a family up to its ears in steak and kidney pudding, grouse and other traditional fare. Although Edward is unusual in liking curry, he is not the first Royal to take an interest in Indian food. Queen Victoria, as Empress of India, felt it her duty to have one curry dish at the dinner 'buffet' (sideboard) every night, so she hired a special Indian chef to provide this, a chap who travelled from India to take up his new position. All the evidence suggests his labours were in vain and that every night his specially-prepared dish of the day was thrown away untouched. That would not have been the case if Edward had been there. He took an early opportunity to sneak Sophie in to the Last Days of the Raj restaurant in Drury Lane. They furtively helped themselves to each other's meals as many couples do — an everyday sign of intimacy. They also loved to swim together in the private Buckingham Palace pool. Sophie had always been a good swimmer. One day while relaxing there she suddenly wondered what would happen if the Queen came in while she was splashing around. 'If the Queen walks in, do I have to curtsy under water?', she asked. Edward thought this was hilarious, although he was sensitive enough to realise that Sophie was more than a little intimidated at meeting his mother.

As with so many couples in the early stages of a relationship, they spent a lot of their time sharing cosy suppers. They enjoyed cooking together and, although Edward's valet would usually prepare supper, they both enjoyed giving him the night off and cooking something themselves. Sophie was particularly adept at quick and easy 'after work' meals like pasta and rice dishes, which single women are used to preparing for a night in front of the telly. Although Edward would pick Sophie up from her flat in Vereker Road he was too conscious of the risk of being seen to spend an evening there. Instead, their private courtship took place in his Buckingham Palace apartment where he could feel safe and relaxed. His rooms had originally been the nursery area for his elder brother Andrew and himself. In many ways it has taken Edward a long time to shake off the ties of childhood. His housekeeper Miss Colebrook still turns down his linen sheets and draws his silk curtains. An article in the London *Evening Standard* in May 1992 claimed he had posters on his walls of himself playing Deputy-Governor Danforth in *The Crucible* at Cambridge and of himself as a wrestler 'The Sandringham Slammer' in *Trafford Tanzi* for The National Youth Theatre. This innocuous revelation evidently peeved the Prince on whose behalf the Buckingham Palace Press office issued stinging denials. This, at a time when everyone was bracing themselves for the forthcoming serialisation of Andrew Morton's *Diana : Her True Story* in the *Sunday Times*.

Most young couples have two anniversaries. The day they met and the day they first did 'it'. Sophie, whose discretion has proved one of her strongest attributes has never let on when she and Edward celebrate that second anniversary. Early in November 1993, about six weeks after they started dating Edward flew to Swaziland on behalf of the Duke of Edinburgh Award Scheme. The old chestnut 'absence makes the heart grow fonder' had never been truer than when the couple were faced with thousands of miles between them. Edward was lonely and miserable in his hotel and the international telephone lines were red hot with 'Gus' calling his sweetheart at all hours of the day. Just before he left he called her to arrange a meeting. Sophie suggested he would be tired when he got back and that they should meet up the day after when he had had a good night's sleep. Edward was not impressed by this concern for his welfare. 'I get in at six o'clock,' he told her. 'I'll pick you up at five past.' Sophie was impressed at the strength of his ardour.

Shortly afterwards Edward suggested they should spend a weekend together at Windsor Castle where Edward had private apartments in The Queen's Tower with a superb position overlooking The Long Walk. The view, however, was not uppermost in Sophie's mind. Edward calmly reassured her that the Queen would be leaving as they arrived, so there was no need to worry about meeting her. This was a small white lie, which members of the Royal Family habitually use to spare guests days of nervous agony wondering what to do and say when they meet the monarch. If you take them by surprise, they do not have time to worry themselves silly. Sophie was considerably surprised when, on the day before they were due to leave for Windsor, Edward told her things had changed and that they would be lunching with the Queen and the Duke of Edinburgh on Sunday. Sophie did not know this at the time, but the Queen does not have a spontaneous life and these events are arranged weeks in advance.

Edward's valet Brian, who was well used to guests making fools of themselves, kindly gave an anxious Sophie some advice on the finer points of sharing a meal with the Royal Family. This is rather like dining on Mars — it's a different world. It was small consolation to Sophie that Edward believes he is in the vanguard of breaking down the social barriers around the Royal Family. In an interview given to that great arbiter of such matters, the *Radio Times* he would later say, 'We are forever being told we have a rigid class structure. That's a load of codswallop.' It is a strident opinion with which the majority of this country might not agree.

Codswallop or not, Sophie's main concern at this point was learning what to do at the end of the meal when the fruit is served. The Royal Family love it when guests make a complete cock-up of this. It is their own private joke. Each person receives a crystal bowl with a knife on top of a napkin placed on a plate. Edward told Sophie that she should remove the bowl for cleansing her hands, put the napkin on her lap and then use the knife and fork for peeling and chopping the various pieces of fruit on offer. Those not in the know spend a number of agonising minutes chasing around bits of peaches and kiwi fruit, which they have mistakenly put in the water for washing their hands.

The big day arrived. Sophie had driven in her old Fiat Panda down to Windsor and, as per Edward's instructions, parked in the courtyard near his apartments. Although she did not fully appreciate them on this occasion, it was obvious that they were far more homely than his rooms at Buckingham Palace. As Malcolm Cockren, Edward's chairman at Ardent told Royal Biographer Ingrid Seward: 'If you see Prince Edward's rooms at Windsor, you know Edward. All the things he likes are there.' And on this occasion the things he liked included one Miss Sophie Rhys-Jones. The apartment is situated on the top floor of The Queen's Tower and has its own private entrance. Sophie immediately felt more relaxed when she started to settle into her own bedroom. There were two bedrooms, two bathrooms and a sitting-room and it would have been bad form for Sophie to park her fluffy slippers underneath Edward's own bed. She was thrilled to have her own maid for her stay. She was called Isabel, a name that had always been lucky for Sophie — the chalet in Crans-Montana had been called Isabella. As most girls would under the circumstances, Sophie brought most of her wardrobe with her. She was determined to be prepared, which was just as well because Edward soon bounced in to tell her they were going riding.

Sophie soon discovered that the great thing about

going riding with the Royals is that the really boring and dirty chores of saddling, brushing and mucking-out are all done for you, so all you have to do is roll up, hop on and trot off. She had never been a great rider and bouncing up and down on a horse did nothing to improve her butterflies. Edward's valet Brian had done his best by assuring her that they would be eating lunch in a particularly large room and that the Queen probably would not speak to her. This was another little white lie to ease Sophie's anxiety. She had chosen a blouse, skirt and jacket for lunch. When she walked in for lunch, the room was tiny and, far from the Queen being a speck at the other end of a huge dining table, it was like being trapped in a lift with the entire cast of *Spitting Image*. The Queen, Prince Philip, Princess Anne and her husband Tim Laurence were all unwinding after attending the Remembrance Day service at the Cenotaph.

The big moment arrived. Edward introduced her to the Queen and the brief handshake and curtsy were over in the blink of an eye. All that practising at Vereker Road had been worth it after all. The lunch itself was a blur. Sophie was sandwiched between Prince Philip and Tim Laurence, but took no part in a conversation that centred on the morning's service and politics in general. She was anxious to create a good impression, but how could she, Sophie Rhys-Jones, make an impression of any kind in this exalted company? She knew enough to keep her mouth firmly shut and concentrate on getting food from the butlers on to her plate. That accomplished, she was too nervous to munch on anything more than a lettuce leaf. The only thing she later recalled about the entire encounter was the Queen dashing over to the window to watch Concorde fly over, dutifully followed by the rest of the family as if they had never seen the plane before. The entire experience was similar to a visit to the dentist —never as bad as you think it's going to be and something you feel pleased with yourself for having done.

When lunch was over Edward suggested a walk in the grounds, taking care not to stray on to the Queen's favoured afternoon route so that he and Sophie could enjoy some time together. They did, however, bump into Andrew and Fergie, then still married, who were bringing the Queen's two grand-daughters Beatrice and Eugenie for tea. Sophie joined them for tea and found the Queen as grandma a far less forbidding prospect. For the first time she chatted politely if a little stiffly with Edward's mother. She was beginning to relax. The Queen was later heard to say of meeting Sophie, 'You wouldn't notice her in a crowd.' This is not as uncomplimentary as it seems. In view of the publicity surrounding the Queen's daughter-in-laws, it was greatly to Sophie's advantage to maintain a low profile and gain the trust of Edward's family.

Nothing could compare with the terror of meeting the Queen socially for the first time. After surviving that ordeal, getting to know the rest of the family was a piece of cake. The week after her first trip to Windsor Castle, she was back again. Edward had been up to Murrayfield to watch the All Blacks against Scotland and had originally planned to stay the weekend, but he could not bear to miss out on seeing Sophie so flew back to take her down to Windsor.

Throughout their courtship, weekends away, usually at Windsor, have become very much the norm for Sophie. Edward would drive them down himself in the green Rover on Friday night and the weekend would officially begin with drinks in the Green Drawing Room followed by dinner in the Oak Drawing Room. The ladies, including the Queen, would wear a simple dress — HM would always wear an expensive string of pearls with hers — and the men would wear lounge suits. Royal men seem to spend 80 per cent of their waking lives in suits. In casual clothes they can appear as uneasy as a goldfish stranded on a hearthrug. Nine times out of ten dinner will be something the Royals have either shot or hooked on the end of a line and guests need to keep a watchful eye for any stray buckshot. Romy Adlington once observed, 'You wouldn't believe how often they eat pheasant, duck paté, roast duck, casserole of grouse or salmon.' Prince Andrew even refers to his sister Anne as the 'smoked salmon housewife' because she serves so many salmon dishes.

Sophie and the other female guests always have breakfast in their rooms, either continental or the full 'English'. Sophie usually has a croissant and some fruit. The best part of the meal is that it is served on a silver tray and brought by a maid or a footman in a Royal livery of black with scarlet lapel and cuffs and shiny silver buttons. Sophie immediately felt like a Queen, or a princess at the very least and, after her initial nerves had been calmed, loved all the pomp. Over the years the staff have become used to the Queen's sons inviting girls for the weekend who have been absolutely terrified of making a social *faux pas*. One girl was so worried about getting mascara on a Royal pillow-case that she brought her own. Another cut her finger while opening the make-up bottle she had bought especially and had hysterics when she dripped blood on a monogrammed towel. A famous tale concerns an old girlfriend of Prince Charles who came across Prince Philip in a corridor wearing a short dressing-gown. She gave one of her very best curtsies only to look up and see a pair of very hairy knees.

Although there are traditional things about a weekend at Windsor such as the Queen serving tea on Sunday with her favourite chocolate cake or helping to pick up the birds after a Sunday shoot, Sophie has always managed to do a little of her own thing like putting on a tracksuit and jogging or swimming in the Castle's solar heated pool. She is, however, very careful not to miss Sunday morning church, which is of paramount importance to the Queen. On her second visit to Windsor she met the Queen Mother when she was invited to join her and the Queen in the Royal Family's private pews at St George's Chapel. She greatly enjoyed that first visit to the chapel — it would be a lovely venue for a wedding.

16

All Hell Let Loose

Sophie's life changed for ever on the morning she met Prince Edward. The next momentous event occurred on an ordinary day at the office. It was late in the afternoon of Friday, 17 December, 1993 and staff at Brian MacLaurin's PR company were getting ready to knock off for the last weekend before Christmas. Sophie was at her desk working on a Press release for Baby Lifeline when a tall, well-built Clark Kent look-a-like strode purposefully up, stood in front of her and loudly announced: 'May I be the first to call you Your Royal Highness the Duchess of Cambridge?' Everyone else in the office was completely stunned. Sophie was shaking down to her boots. The tall dark stranger was Royal author Andrew Morton, who had achieved fame and fortune with his revelations about the Princess of Wales in *Diana: Her True Story*. Morton had started off in Fleet Street as a run-of-the-mill news reporter on the downmarket *Daily Star*, so a bit of old-style foot in the door was no problem for him. He has had to get used to the Clark Kent jibes over the years but on this occasion he proved to be not so much Superman as Houdini because he had to get past two security doors to find his way to Sophie.

Fortunately for Sophie, her boss Brian MacLaurin was at work during this crisis. He had met Morton once before in the office of the then *Sun* editor Stuart Higgins, so he knew who he was and also knew it could mean big trouble. 'I quickly realised I couldn't put Morton's arm up his back and put him through the door. Besides the fact that he's a foot taller than me, I'm a PR man and this is a PR company. So I did the most sensible thing I could think of and separated them. I took Sophie, shaking, into the board-room to calm down while I went out to deal with Morton.'

'Andrew, what is it you are here to do?' said Brian innocently. 'Don't bullshit me,' said Morton. 'I've got photographs of them together. I've got friends who saw them at the theatre.' He proceeded to give Sophie's boss chapter and verse on her relationship with Prince Edward. Although Brian had a vague idea about the private friendship that had sprung up, the details were news to him. He was agog and privately was dying to hear all the details. Still, with great professionalism all he said to Morton was a simple 'Fine' and went back to Sophie. He told her that Morton had pictures of her and Edward at her flat the previous night. He ran through what Morton had, so she couldn't deny it and then proceeded to write her a statement. Morton was called in and Sophie read it to him: 'Prince Edward and I are good friends and we work together. He is a private person and so am I. I have nothing more to add.'

After that it was a chance for everyone to take a breath. Morton had got his quote and could happily think of the loot he would get from the Sunday papers for this scoop. They all had a coffee and he told Sophie that he was not going to carve her up. Instead, he gave her some hints about how to deal with the onslaught and what to do when confronted by the paparazzi — something she would have to face up to for the rest of her life. He also promised not to let on where her parents lived, although even Sophie must have realised that it would take the rest of Fleet Street all of two minutes to find that out. All Sophie could think of to say as Morton prepared to leave was 'please don't say my hair is ginger.' He didn't. 'Andrew Morton was very decent,' observed Brian MacLaurin at a later date.

What to do next? The first thing for Sophie was to ring Edward and tell him what had happened. They decided that Brian would drive her to Hampton Court where Edward's car would be waiting to meet her. The couple often rendezvoused there to play real tennis with their friend and coach Lesley Ronaldson. In any case, Sophie already had a bag in the office ready for a weekend at Windsor. These Castle breaks had now become part of their regular routine and were the highlight of Sophie's week. Brian and Sophie sped off over Hammersmith Bridge in his silver Mazda sports car, hotly pursued by three leather-clad men on motorbikes. It was quite obvious they were being followed. The ensuing chase through West London was like something out of *The Sweeney* with Brian roaring down Castelnau, through Roehampton before cutting left into Dover House Road. It was very exciting. A breathless Sophie spent the drive on the phone to Edward in his car telling him exactly what was happening as they managed to lose their pursuers by doubling back by Roehampton Church. They later found out that the three bikers were photographers from the *News of the World*. At Hampton Court the familiar green Rover was waiting and Sophie was off quicker than a photographer's flash. The couple, whose romance would never be the same again, drove off to spend the weekend at Windsor Castle.

Saturday was a day spent on tenterhooks. The Queen was informed of the development and warned to expect some revelations in the Sunday papers. She was well used to them and told Sophie that this was the downside of being associated with her family. As usual, Edward and Sophie spent the afternoon walking around the grounds. They had much to think about. Edward was angry that they had lost their privacy through no fault of their own. He was furious that his private business was now in the public domain and that the journalist responsible was Andrew Morton whose book on Diana would, in earlier times, have consigned him to a lengthy stay in the Tower of London. For her part, as she later confided to friends, Sophie was worried that she would be placed at arms' length for the foreseeable future because of Edward's great aversion to the Press. Sunday arrived and with it the unusual sight of a neatly pressed copy of the *News of the World* on Edward's breakfast tray. EDWARD IN LOVE it proclaimed in a huge banner headline. 'A Christmas romance to touch your heart' and 'Sophie set to be Royal bride next summer' were the secondary headlines. It could have been much worse.

As with the majority of Royal stories, some of Andrew Morton's 'Royal Scoop of the Year' was true and some of it was not. The first paragraph read: 'Prince Edward is in love and ready to marry the girl of his dreams next year.' Well, Edward was deeply in love with Sophie, but there was to be no quickstep up the aisle. Morton also suggested they would announce a spring engagement on 30 March, Edward's 30th birthday, followed by a televised summer wedding at Westminster Abbey. And that Edward would become the Duke of Cambridge. None of this happened, although one could speculate on whether it would have if their romance had been granted more time to develop before becoming public property.

The most eye-catching detail that the millions of *News of the World* readers could take in on that chilly December morning was that Sophie had spent the night at Buckingham Palace. As Morton so memorably put it: 'I counted Sophie out of her West London flat, I did not count her back again.' The implication that theirs was already a sexual relationship was quite clear and, if nothing else, it gave Edward some heterosexual street cred to think that he did not spend every night cuddling his teddy bear.

There's only one thing worse than a newspaper scoop: the follow-ups. Because, while a scoop is normally undertaken in secret by just one or two journalists, the follow-up is a free-for-all as the other papers try to catch up. It becomes something akin to a pack of jackals slavering over the carcass of a fallen deer after the lion has had its fill. Edward, who had seen his family take some shattering body blows, realised that without great care his relationship with Sophie could be torn apart. Morton could retire gracefully to his luxurious London home and watch the pack get on with it.

Sophie cheerily suggested that no one would be that interested in the news that Edward had a girlfriend. The daily diet of Diana and Fergie stories was a big enough Royal meal for anyone. It would not be long before she was shown to be wide of the mark. She was, however, able to soothe some of Edward's annoyance, something at which she has become very accomplished. Sophie, although Andrew Morton's intrusion into her life had been most unwelcome, was determined to be the rock on which Edward could rely.

On Sunday evening she left Windsor and stayed that night at Brian MacLaurin's Surrey home so that he could drive her into work. They decided to get there bright and early before the Press were up and running. They arrived at the office at 6.45am. Three television crews and 50 or 60 photographers and reporters were waiting — more than Sophie had ever seen in her life. So much for a lack of interest. The office security guards, faced with this invasion, had closed the gates. What the assembled massed ranks of Her Majesty's Press did not know was that Sophie was no longer wearing her hair in the style displayed in the *News of the World*. They had used a photo from that first meeting at Queen's Club, but in October Sophie had had her hair restyled at Edward's suggestion into a smart blonde bob. She had also lost weight, as often happens to girls in love. The chic young woman in the passenger seat of Brian MacLaurin's car was not immediately recognisable as the Brenchley Belle. Certainly none of the photographers or reporters recognised her as they huddled around in the pouring rain. Arthur Edwards of the *Sun*, almost the doyen of Royal snappers, put his head though the car window and said, 'Morning, Brian'. Kenny Lennox, just promoted to *Sun* picture editor, knew Brian MacLaurin from their Glasgow days. He cheerily put his head in the other side of the car and asked, 'Where have you put her, Brian, in the boot?'

As the gates opened Brian looked across at Lennox and said 'Kenny!' and pointed at Sophie. 'You should have seen the look on his face,' recalled Brian, chuckling. 'I drove off into the underground car park and not one flashbulb had gone off.'

The phones in the office were burning hot. Kenny, Arthur, the world and his wife were ringing up pleading for a picture. Sophie told Brian that she was not going out. After a couple of hours, pressure was building at the London *Evening Standard* and the early news bulletins. Brian MacLaurin, ever the hard-nosed PR man, realised that they had to do something because the *News of the World* had carried a very significant story. His name would also be mud if the Press got nothing. So he phoned Prince Edward who unhelpfully suggested that he tell the Press to go away. Brian respectfully said that he could not do that because Sophie was in his office, this was his company and he had to continue dealing with the very people who were outside. Edward saw sense and told Brian to say he had spoken to him, they were good friends and please leave Sophie and him alone. Brian and Sophie then had a chat and it was agreed that he would go out and pass on Edward's remarks to the reporters. After asking for hush he told the hacks that he had spoken to Edward and Sophie and that they had asked 'could you give us a break?'

Two hours later the *Evening Standard* hit the London streets with a front-page splash proclaiming EDWARD : GIVE US A BREAK. In the meantime Brian MacLaurin had to field questions from an impatient mob shouting: 'Is marriage imminent?' 'Absolutely not,' said Brian, firmly. 'This is a young relationship. Give them a break. They need some space.' Brian then gave a few brief interviews stating what a fantastic person Sophie was which kept the journalists happy as the rain cascaded down on London W14. Unknown to Mr MacLaurin, Prince Edward was simultaneously preparing a letter to the Press, echoing the request for him and Sophie to be given time and privacy to develop their relationship. At least he didn't hide behind the trite denials of the Buckingham Palace Press Office, which over the years had perfected a thousand and one ways to say absolutely nothing. Instead Edward had talked it over with his friend and PR advisor Abel Hadden, whose wife Belinda was to become so helpful to Sophie. Edward had littered the original copy with some heavy-handed sarcasm, but was persuaded to tone down the published version. He settled for saying, 'I am very conscious that other members of my family have been subjected to similar attention and it has not been at all beneficial to their relationships.' This simplistic view of the famous *annus horribilis* was, unintentionally, quite funny.

Meanwhile Sophie had to face for the first time something that she would grow very accustomed to — the clicking of cameras all pointing at her. She has always enjoyed posing for photographs, but there was a world of difference between happy holiday snaps and having a Nikon shoved up your nose. Brian MacLaurin went out with a tray of teas and coffees to let the media foot soldiers know what was happening. He and his staff were about to leave to go to their office Christmas party — the ruination of the MacLaurin Communication and Media Limited Christmas party was to become an annual occurrence. At this stage the police arrived to erect riot barriers, so that a casual observer might have thought the Pope was expected — not Sophie Rhys-Jones from Brenchley.

Sophie came out of the office next to Brian MacLaurin. As they reached the bank of photographers, Brian dropped back enabling everyone to get a clear shot of their prey. Before she got into the car Sophie stopped, looking straight at the photographers, counted to three and then got in. She made it. In fact, everyone agreed that she did brilliantly. The entire day had been excellent PR for Sophie and didn't do Brian MacLaurin any harm either. Sophie's lifelong interest in acting saw her through on this occasion, as it would do many times in the future.

Andrew Morton, quite correctly, has never revealed the source of his story. In a later article in *OK!* he revealed that the prime suspects for the leak were either police or staff at Windsor Castle. It is therefore pretty safe to assume the source of the leak was definitely NOT police or staff at Windsor Castle. It is far more likely that Morton wants everyone to believe the mole is a Royal one when in all probability it is someone who knows Sophie in some capacity. There is nothing to be gained by Morton letting on who it was, as that might jeopardise future scoops from that particular source.

There is no doubt who was originally fingered as the source of the scoop — Edward was convinced it was the Duchess of York. At that time, both Fergie and Diana were seen as incorrigible Press blabs by the Palace Old Guard. One can't forget a topless Fergie had been seen having her toes caressed and sucked by John Bryan who had been dubbed by the Press as her 'financial adviser'. It would certainly remove some of the heat from Fergie should a new media interest be developed at the Palace. Edward was and remains fiercely loyal to his brothers. Although he initially warmed to the new blood in the family and found both Diana and Fergie a breath of fresh air, he firmly believed Sarah Ferguson had made a fool of Andrew. Edward sent a memo to his elder brother accusing the Duchess of spilling the beans about Sophie and was somewhat taken aback to receive a frosty response that Sarah was completely innocent. For her part Fergie complained directly to the Queen that she was blameless and after a private meeting with his mother Edward apologised for any upset — to the Queen of course, not to Fergie.

The Prince did, however, do something in the wake of his love affair becoming public knowledge. His office circulated a memo marked Top Secret, which, rather typically, fell into Andrew Morton's hands. It began: 'The story now running in the Press plus the Andrew Morton involvement means things will not quieten down for a while.' This proved to be correct, although you did not have to be a rocket scientist to realise that this would be the case. The memo went out to, among others, Sophie and her parents warning them not to use mobile phones or put their rubbish out the night before it was due to be collected. The prospect of unnamed Sunday newspaper hacks rifling through the rubbish bags outside Vereker Road to see what sort of cereal they ate or the brand of shampoo they used reduced Sophie and her flatmate Ulli to tears of laughter. The memo also suggested the best way of dealing with the paparazzi: 'If they turn up at your home, send them out a cup of tea. If it's Christmas, send them a cracker.' Although Sophie chuckled at it in private she knew that when Edward was in pompous mode she had to treat him with care and deadly seriousness.

The attentions of the Press were an entirely new experience for Sophie's parents but they handled it well, particularly her father who decided that there was nothing to be gained by being unfriendly. He told his local paper, 'Sophie was upset in the beginning by all the media attention because she just wants a quiet life. She is a normal girl who has had a normal life. She grew up around here and did all the things that little girls do. She loves the theatre and loved learning ballet as a child. After doing a typing course near here she left to make her fortune in London as girls often do and has been having a great time ever since.' And that is basically all he has ever had to say on the subject having been well advised by Sophie that the best comment you can ever make is no comment.

Although Sophie was wise enough to realise that, on the memorable day when Andrew Morton had strode into her office, she had been dumped in the middle of a minefield with possible disaster at every step, privately she was relieved. Keeping the secret from the majority of her friends had taxed even her considerable will power. Just two days before 'all hell let loose' she had bumped into old boyfriend Andrew Parkinson and had somehow managed to keep it to herself. The publicity had to happen sometime. After all, she was Prince Edward's girlfriend and she was proud of that.

17

A Norfolk Broad

The sleepy village of Brenchley was in a flurry of excitement. Nothing like this had ever happened. As planned, Sophie came home for a family Christmas, probably the last normal one she would ever have. Displaying the trait that makes the British middle classes so great, everyone she met was polite and friendly but made a deliberate point of not asking her, 'How's Eddie?' even though they were consumed with curiosity. It has always been considered the height of bad manners to be nosy to one's face. If Mick Jagger had walked into Sophie's local, everyone would have moved heaven and earth to pretend it was no big deal. Nobody would start humming 'Honky Tonk Women'. And so it was with Sophie. She was the chief topic of conversation over the Christmas festivities, but when she and her parents popped to the local for some seasonal cheer all the talk was of trivial village gossip.

Her parents Christopher and Mary have lived in the

village for 30 years and are part of the furniture there. A local resident and friend summed up the attitude of the village: 'There is an unwritten bond to protect the Rhys-Jones. They are a very respected part of the community.' Sophie's parents were naturally bursting with pride for their daughter, but they were also very worried for her future following the Press speculation. They had met Edward when their daughter had invited her new boyfriend down for Sunday lunch. They found him very easy to get along with and happy to join them for a walk around the village. Being the parents of a Royal girlfriend, especially a serious one, is not an easy role for one simple reason — nobody ever tells you anything. The late Mrs Anne Phillips, the mother of Captain Mark Phillips, lamented after her son was engaged to Princess Anne, 'The Palace never tells us what is going on. We feel like complete outsiders.' In the meantime her parents were almost as excited about everything as Sophie. Her father merrily joked to friends about Edward's 'prospects' and having to hock the family silver for the wedding at Westminster Abbey. It was all very jolly, but the limelight was entirely new to the Rhys-Jones family and not entirely welcome.

It had already been arranged that Sophie would see in 1994 at Sandringham where the New Year's House Party was a famous social occasion. To receive a Sandringham invitation you must first pass the Windsor Castle Sunday lunch test with flying colours, which Sophie had done. Sandringham House, a mock-Jacobean mansion in north Norfolk that Edward VII acquired as the Prince of Wales in 1862, is one of the Queen's two resplendent private homes. The other is Balmoral where the family take their traditional August break. In January they all decamp to

Sandringham for the pheasant shooting and some lavish entertaining. Sophie drove herself up from Brenchley on New Year's Eve via the M25 and A10, a distance of about 150 miles.

Most of the guests at these occasions are regulars and have been friends of the Queen for years. The younger Royals could bring boyfriends or girlfriends, but the emphasis is very much on a relaxed atmosphere. The basic rules of Royal protocol, however, are always observed even if the guests have known the Queen for 60 years. They still curtsy or bow when she comes into a room or if they meet her in a corridor and they never leave a room before her. Sophie was by now *au fait* with most of the regal rules and found them second nature. 'It's just like being at school,' she told a close friend. 'If you think of the Queen as the headmistress you can't go far wrong.'

The front door of Sandringham opens into a large hall, a bit like a hotel foyer with lots of comfortable chairs scattered around. The furniture is definitely for sitting and snoozing in and not the sort of 'look but don't touch' ornate antiques you see on a guided tour of Buckingham Palace. Just inside the front door, which has screens around it to keep out the bitterly cold Norfolk winds, are a pair of sitting scales that look rather like buckets. They were installed at the request of King Edward VII who liked to weigh all his guests when they arrived and again when they left to see how many pounds they had put on while feasting at his table. Needless to say Sophie had to take her turn in the bucket, which was a bit embarrassing as a girl never wants her partner to know her exact weight (nine stone). It was a giggle though. There is also a piano where Princess Margaret likes to play and lead the evening sing-song plus a card table and lots of magazines, although the Queen is not too keen on old copies of *Hello!* that feature her ex-daughter-in-law, the Duchess of York.

The hall opens up to a height of two floors and, from a well-chosen vantage point, the Queen can sit and watch guests roll up in their cars. She was there to see Sophie arrive in her clapped-out white Fiat Panda. One of the great traditions of Sandringham in January is a giant jigsaw puzzle that is laid out over two card tables, so that guests and family can amuse themselves if it's raining or they are first back from a ride. There is an unwritten law that if a guest should deprive the Queen of the thrill of finishing the holiday jigsaw, they can expect a bed to be made up for them in The Tower of London. The jigsaws are provided free by toy companies. One black year the Queen was excitedly finishing off a particularly difficult landscape when she triumphantly prepared to insert the final piece. Only there was no sign of it. Servants were summoned and the room turned upside down until a fuming monarch stormed off. A message of strong complaint was dispatched via her Private Secretary's office to the manufacturers. To save their necks they sent round a replacement straight away, having first completed it themselves to make sure it was satisfactory.

Usually the ballroom is laid out for the Saturday night film. After dinner all the houseguests are expected to attend and they sit in comfortable armchairs and sofas. The Queen and Prince Philip have the best seats in the 'centre stalls'. There are nearly always two or three soon-to-be released movies to choose from and it's considered a sign of great social cachet to say, 'I saw that one up at Sandringham.' It is much better attended than a small town cinema on a dreary Monday afternoon. All the staff can bring their families, although they are expected to sit in 'rear stalls' on collapsible director-style canvas chairs. The rule is that you have to be in your seat before the Queen arrives. One of the servants acts as a projectionist while an equerry is positioned near the Queen ready to alert him if she thinks the sound is too loud or too low. Afterwards guests help themselves to a night-cap from a drinks tray so that everyone can chat about the film before going to bed.

During New Year, the film is traditionally the black-and-white classic *The Hound of the Baskervilles* to please Edward's father. He loves it and talks the whole way through as if he is part of the action while the rest of the audience gently doze. For the rest of the family the screening ranks second to the Royal Variety Show on the snoozometer. Right on cue as Sherlock Holmes closes in on the villain, Philip springs from his seat and shouts, 'Oh for God's sake, man, get on with it!' It's the same every year.

On New Year's Eve the ballroom is converted back to its original purpose, although one feature remains a fixture — Edward's VII's huge collection of creaky old armour. You can easily imagine somebody hiding in the iron suit as if in some B-movie horror flick. Sophie was by now becoming accustomed to two facts of life about Royal invitations. First, the visit almost always began with a ride. And second, she needed about five outfits per day. Riding, shooting, lunch, tea and dinners. The only time you did not have to dress up was at breakfast, which guests were always served in their room. New Year's Eve was black tie, of course, so Sophie had to find a new ballgown for the night.

Edward collected her for the pre-dinner drinks in the drawing-room. Sophie was handed a large dry martini specially mixed by an equerry. The measures are generous, but the trick is to make your drink last. It would be very bad form to get drunk even on New Year's Eve, although, on the odd occasion when this has happened, the Queen pretends not to notice. The problem with being nervous is that you can easily gulp down your drinks, although at New Year the guests tend to be regulars and at ease with the occasion. There is always someone at your elbow to fill or refill your glass. Edward, who doesn't have much practice of helping himself, is hopeless at pouring drinks and always mixes far too strong a measure — something Sophie has become adept at avoiding. It is common knowledge that Princess Margaret and the Queen Mum enjoy a tipple or two, but the Queen never gets drunk. She might, on New Year's Eve, get a little 'giggly'.

The night itself is one of old-fashioned gaiety with laughing, drinking, dancing and a rousing rendition of 'Auld Lang Syne'. Edward and Sophie were happy to be back in the comfortable cocoon of friends and family after the glare of the media spotlight had taken some of the magic away from their affair. Edward was determined that Sophie should not be cast in the role of a passing flight of fancy. This was by far the most serious relationship of his life and he wanted it to last. Edward does, however, have a complex view of the Press. Yes, it is tinged with something close to paranoia, but he is also as obstinate as a mule and the very last thing he would want is to appear to have been pushed into anything by the media. He was faced, therefore, with a double jeopardy problem at this point. He wanted to show Sophie the strength of his feelings and to reassure her that they could stand firm against public scrutiny. On the other hand he did not want anyone to know. The solution was that the couple had a delightful New Year's Eve and came to an 'understanding' that they were unofficially engaged. Edward convinced Sophie that they should be seen to be conducting their own private lives and not being steamrollered by outside influences.

More than two years later when *Radio Times* journalist Andrew Duncan asked him about his intentions, the tetchy Prince snapped: 'If you shut up, mind your own business and let me do it when I want, it is much more likely to happen.' The key phrase there is 'when I want'. He did not say ' when *we* want'. Sophie has been content not to rush things and just to enjoy the flowering of their friendship, a course of action that has been warmly and sympathetically received by the Queen who had also suffered the uncertainty of an unofficial engagement. That was in late 1946 when she was madly in love with the dashing naval officer Philip Mountbatten, but had to overcome the resistance of her father King George VI and of the Buckingham Palace establishment. The King did not want to lose the eldest daughter he adored and the courtiers considered the future Prince Philip unsuitable despite his Royal blood. In fact the senior courtier Sir Alan Lascelles, the King's Private Secretary confided to his friend, the royal biographer Harold Nicholson, that they feared Philip was 'rough, uneducated and would probably not be faithful'. That view seems incredible now. In the end it took Elizabeth and Philip a year to persuade the King to allow their marriage.

The support of the Queen and Prince Philip has been evident from the early days. Edward talked to his mother in secret about wanting to choose the right time to be married and not to be rushed into things by the media or the Palace machine. The Queen was sympathetic and agreed to any arrangement Edward and Sophie might make, provided that it was understood that they would eventually marry.

As a result, Sophie has benefitted from the full weight of the Queen's approval. She was allowed to travel to church in the same car as the Queen. This is a privilege that is afforded only to someone 'engaged' to a member of the family. Serena Linley, for instance, was not allowed to do this until she and Viscount Linley had formally declared their intentions. Lord Linley's former long-standing girlfriend, Susannah Constantine, who was very popular with the Royals, was never given this honour. Nor was Diana Spencer. Church-going remains a very important aspect of the Queen's life. She never misses church on Sunday. Sandringham is no exception. It is not compulsory for guests to attend, but they are discreetly told that the Queen 'prefers' it if they do. Princess Margaret is usually in bed when everyone else is singing lustily.

In many ways the past two weeks had marked a watershed for Sophie. She was unofficially engaged to one of the most eligible men in the world and she could not tell a soul. Only her parents and her very closest friends knew the situation. No one at work was told. As Brian MacLaurin observed, 'It is very difficult for Sophie. Here's a fun-loving girl who finds herself projected into the spotlight wherever she goes and that has inevitably made her clam up. She is now very cautious about what she says, very quiet about certain things and very discreet. Until it goes any further she has to maintain the position that she is an ordinary person going about her life.'

Everyone is quite clear on one point where Sophie is concerned — she has enormous powers of discretion and she has needed them as she has adjusted to her new-found status as a celebrity because assuredly that is what the Royal Family are in this day and age. Her friend and colleague Nick Skeens remembers travelling by train to jobs with Sophie when her guard would relax just a little. He recalls: 'She was like a young girl who had suddenly entered a bit of a fairy-tale world and all of a sudden these people out of a fairy tale were real people. The Queen was suddenly just a mother. And Prince Charles was just a potential brother-in-law. And Prince Andrew was just a potential brother-in-law. She said she felt she had entered an unreal world, but that unreal world had a common or garden reality. It was all a big roller-coaster ride. She was off on this incredible adventure. She gave me the impression that suddenly she had been hitched up to this great, big rock 'n' rolling ride to a whole new world. She was in awe of her new life, but enthralled by it. I found it fascinating how she adapted to what is an incredible lifestyle, one that other people can only dream about. It's a lottery win many times over.'

Sophie's roller-coaster ride included the daily routine of coping with paparazzi hanging around outside her office waiting to snap her scurrying into work. Leanne Tritton-Jones, who worked with Sophie at MacLaurin Communications, says Sophie coped by being completely normal. 'If I was going to get a sandwich from the local deli for lunch she would come, too, and walk up with me. A few people would look up as we walked down the street because everyone knew who she was, but she didn't or wouldn't notice. We would go into the deli and have a normal chat.' One thing changed right away. Up until the Andrew Morton revelations Sophie had parked in the street. Brian MacLaurin saw to it that she had a pass for the underground car park, so that she could drive instead of having to walk past the paparazzi every morning, unlike Leanne and her colleagues. That ploy failed on one occasion when Sophie left her car on a yellow line while she dashed into the office for a minute. During that minute she was given a parking ticket, much to the amusement of the few paparazzi who were trailing her. Photographer Andrew Murray recalls, 'We moved the ticket so that when she got in she couldn't see out of the windscreen so she had to get out to take the ticket off, and then we all got the picture. It was one of the funniest pictures we ever did.'

Sophie's 29th birthday fell on 30 January. This was the first chance that Prince Edward had to give her a personal token of his love away from prying family eyes who devour every present at Christmas-time. It would have been the perfect time to slip into Garrards, the Royal jewellers, and select a discreet diamond especially after the drama of the past month. Instead, Edward chose a suitcase. It was a very nice suitcase and Edward had gone to the trouble of having her initials engraved on the outside. It was, however, when push comes to shove just a suitcase and hardly designed to sweep a girl off her feet. A disappointed Sophie was faced with having to answer her friends' eager question, 'What did Edward give you?' with the far from impressive words 'A jolly nice suitcase'. In fact, pieces of jewellery have never featured in presents between Edward and Sophie. The only time the Press have noticed Sophie wearing something new was later that year in October when she sported a teddy-bear brooch. The papers declared it to be diamond-encrusted and to have cost Edward a cool £12,000. It was actually a little prezzie that had been given to Sophie by a child at one of her charity events.

The suitcase present shows Edward in an

unromantic light, which does not do justice to his true nature. A friend, who has seen letters written to Sophie, confides that he calls her 'Darling' and signs off 'with masses of love, Edward', with four kisses and two hearts at the end. He can be very romantic, but he is also quite inexperienced in affairs of the heart. Sophie has found that he can be incredibly thoughtful one minute and totally thoughtless the next. He does not do it on purpose. Like many men he just does not think. He will bombard Sophie with phonecalls declaring his love, he will send her huge bunches of roses as he did just a couple of weeks later on Valentine's Day, he will take her away for incredibly romantic weekends in the most beautiful locations. And he will buy her a suitcase for her birthday.

On the evening of her birthday Edward and Sophie had planned a quiet supper at his place. Edward had phoned to say he would be late as he was meeting a television producer and so it was a grumpy Miss Rhys-Jones who arrived at his apartment. There was a forlorn bunch of balloons tied to the back of a chair, but she could not see any sign of the supper. Suddenly the door was flung open. 'Surprise!' shouted a gang of her best friends as they rushed in followed by an ebullient Edward. Sophie had absolutely no idea of Edward's plans and she was absolutely thrilled. Just when she was feeling disappointed and disgruntled, her prince had turned up trumps with the most wonderful surprise. It's not every girl that has her birthday party at Buckingham Palace. At the end of the evening when the guests had gone and they were alone together Edward sheepishly produced a second present. It was an antique silver frame containing a photograph of Edward from his days as a Marine. A happy Sophie promised to keep it by her bed and that's where it sits to this day. A friend of Sophie's best summed it up, 'Edward *is* romantic but he is also Royal. But you should see the glint in her eye when she speaks of him.'

Edward was well aware of Sophie's prowess as a skier. If you have been a ski rep you are bound to be good mainly because you get so much practice. Ski writer Arnie Wilson says that the Duchess of York would come top of any Royal skiing league. Her time with Paddy McNally in Switzerland, when there was not much else to do other than ski, has given her a head start over the rest. Prince Charles is also accomplished and has a daredevil streak in him where sport is concerned. Sophie is certainly a better skier than Edward and would be near the top of the list. For their first real holiday together they decided to take a winter break at St Anton, a resort Edward had always enjoyed as a boy. Just before they were due to leave Edward cancelled the entire thing because Diana was going to the neighbouring resort of Lech with William and Harry. Edward thought so many Royals in close proximity would be like a red rag to a bull for the paparazzi, although the snappers would have had eyes only for Diana.

Sophie was heartbroken that their first holiday together was finished before it had begun. Rather than sit at home feeling miserable Edward suggested they fly up to Scotland and stay at Craigowan Lodge, five minutes' walk among towering pine trees from Balmoral. It is a place steeped in romance where the Royal Family are concerned. The six-bedroomed 'country cottage' was originally built for Queen Victoria's private secretaries, but has now become a sort of Royal honeymoon hotel. Princess Anne and Mark Phillips announced their engagement there and she then went one better with Commander Tim Laurence by spending her wedding night at the lodge. The Duke and Duchess of Kent also spent their honeymoon among the tartan carpets and simple pine furniture. Charles took Diana there before they got married and when they were still talking to one another. Sophie adored the place. It is not exactly Spartan because there is a sauna and satellite television. Best of all, though, the young couple had the 50,000 acre Balmoral estate almost to themselves. Sophie is at her happiest in the country, not among the traffic fumes of Hammersmith Broadway. Although she never breathes a word about the intimate details of her relationship with Edward, she cannot help herself when it comes to the wonderful weekends and cosy breaks they share around the country. This is when the couple's relationship is at its strongest.

Craigowan Lodge was unfortunately the venue for one of those occasions when Edward could no longer control his enormous mistrust and hatred of the Press — the infamous kite-flying pictures. These were a not particularly interesting set of long-lens photographs showing Edward and Sophie messing about with a large yellow kite. In one Sophie has fallen over on her bottom. In another they are sharing an innocent kiss. They are completely harmless and show the couple to be perfectly happy and relaxed. Edward went bananas when they appeared in the national newspapers and made a formal complaint to the Press Complaints Commission, a piece of poor judgement. Sophie who knows the business well has proved to be much more adaptable than Edward, although to be fair his general demeanour has improved as their relationship goes from strength to strength.

The Commission upheld the complaint and the

newspapers apologised half-heartedly, except the *Sun* which took the opportunity to call Edward a 'pompous, petulant and precious prig'. Edward, realising he had transformed a light breeze into a hurricane, withdrew his complaint and instead invited all the Fleet Street editors to Buckingham Palace to discuss the issue of press intrusion. This was against the advice of senior Palace aides who shrewdly counselled that Daniel should not invite the lions into his sleeping quarters. In the end only two editors attended the discussion because of the sad death the same day of Labour leader John Smith and Edward's agenda fizzled out like a damp squib.

Edward would be 30 at the beginning of March and Sophie decided she would like to repay the favour of her own surprise birthday party by organising one for her prince. From humble beginnings the 'surprise' party soon escalated into one of the social events of the year. And Sophie was lumbered with organising it all. It was not exactly a surprise because the Queen herself paid Sophie a huge compliment by putting in an appearance at The Savoy, the venue she had chosen after long and careful consideration. She had decided that somewhere in the West End would be better for Edward's many theatrical friends. For the menu she chose smoked salmon filled with smoked trout and avocado followed by mussel soup. The main course was fillets of lamb with dauphinoise potatoes and spinach (to keep up Edward's strength). Pudding was a chocolate cup filled with pecan ice-cream. It was a huge success and everyone congratulated Sophie on a marvellous party. And then came the bill for £2,000. The prospect of having to nip into the kitchens of The Savoy and do £2,000 worth of washing-up was not one that greatly appealed to Sophie. Fortunately Michael

Cockron, chairman of Edward's television company Ardent Productions, discreetly spared her financial blushes and all was well. It would never have occurred to Edward that money could be a problem for anyone he knew. It is not that he is ungenerous. He just would never realise. He had, however, already noted approvingly that Sophie was prudent with her cash, not appreciating that she had to be.

18

Press-Ganged

S ophie's worst ordeal since she started going out with Edward proved not to be meeting his mother nor looking up from her desk to see the imposing figure of Andrew Morton striding across the office. No, the worst day was 27 June, 1994 — the day that James Whitaker of the *Daily Mirror* told the world that the romance was over. IT'S OFF proclaimed the *Mirror's* front page. Her boss Brian MacLaurin recalls, 'The first Sophie heard about it was on the car radio on her way to meet me for a Press call. She was genuinely very upset.' As we now know the cheerful and chubby Whitaker had, not for the first time, got it completely wrong. The dilemma for Sophie was that on that summer morning she had been taken completely by surprise by his 'Royal exclusive'. Was this how members of the Royal Family ditch their girlfriends, leaking a 'Dear John' letter to the Press?

By the time that Sophie arrived to join Brian MacLaurin at what was expected to be a very lightly attended event at Wycombe Air Park in Buckinghamshire, it had turned into a giant media circus. It was the last thing she needed, but she was able to turn it to her advantage with a little help from Brian who wrote her a speech. Once more she transformed herself into an actress at Brenchley Amateur Dramatics. She was calm, collected and smiling broadly when she told the Press: 'One of the reasons why I actually enjoy working with you guys is that I don't know what I'm going to read next.' It was perfect and went down very well with Edward who also decided to laugh off the *Daily Mirror* story. Sophie then proceeded to be happy and vivacious as she mixed with Noel Edmonds, Tony Blackburn and Mr Blobby at the event, which was in aid of 4,000 disabled children.

The following day, the newspapers all carried Sophie's smiling denial that there was anything wrong in her relationship with Edward. DON'T MAKE ME LAUGH shouted the *Sun*, happy to promote the suggestion that the *Mirror*'s exclusive was rubbish. It was all part of the learning process for Sophie. As Brian MacLaurin wryly observed, 'I have never met James Whitaker. I understand he quotes me and I heard him on GMTV one morning talking about me as if he knew me, but I have never met him in my life. I am told he is a lovely man.'

Sophie's mother Mary, who was monitoring the romance as keenly as any mum would, saw the *Daily Mirror* story. Family friend Patricia Heaney, who lives in Brenchley, noted, 'I know she was deeply upset when the newspapers said the relationship was off. She immediately telephoned Sophie, but she didn't want to interfere and ask her directly about the story. So it was never mentioned. Mary took it that if Sophie didn't mention it then it probably wasn't true. Mary then told the rest of the village not to believe everything they read. She said: "I spoke to Sophie and she mentioned nothing to me. She was her normal self."'

In Whitaker's defence rumours about Edward and Sophie had been doing the rounds since she failed to show for Royal Ascot earlier in the month. The couple may well have had the odd rocky patch as Sophie struggled to cope with the constant media glare since Morton had told the world of their affair. She also found her position as secret fiancée increasingly frustrating. Typically after the *Daily Mirror* story there was a flurry of Press coverage showing them to be a happy couple and very much together.

It was not exactly an orchestrated campaign, but even suspicious old Edward saw that it was the best way for them to get on with their lives. First, it was reported that Sophie's mother and father would be joining the Queen at Balmoral in August. This gave a sort of Royal approval to the fact that Edward and Sophie were still together. Then they attended the wedding of Princess Margaret's daughter Sarah Armstrong Jones and Daniel Chatto, which gave rise to some good-humoured 'will they be next?' thoughts in the newspapers. Next up was what was described as Sophie's first royal engagement. The Royal Tournament in Earls Court might not be most young women's first choice for a night out but, on this occasion, it offered just the right blend of solid respectability and photo opportunity. Edward is patron of the annual military jamboree and arrived first for the official introductions. Sophie and some friends joined him later with a police escort — a further sign of official recognition. Sophie chose a bright and shiny gold designer jacket, which looked more like something Liz Hurley or Princess Diana would have worn. In other words, it guaranteed a prominent picture. Sophie sat behind Edward and he made a point of turning round and whispering amusing asides to her, although there are not too many belly laughs at the Royal Tournament. Sophie felt very important.

Although these three things — her parents' invitation to Balmoral, the wedding of Sarah Armstrong Jones and The Royal Tournament — may not appear a big deal in the great maelstrom of the Royal Family they represented a breakthrough for Sophie. Up until James Whitaker's story Sophie had been presented only as Edward's girlfriend. Now, in the all-important eyes of the public, they were a Royal couple. It was a huge step. Now, just one more piece of the jigsaw was needed to cast Whitaker's story to the dustbin: Edward and Sophie had to be seen as a happy and loving couple. It's all very well saying everything is all right and turning up together at a Royal function, but Charles and Diana fooled no one when they did that. The perfect opportunity came just a few days later — Cowes sailing week. For once there were more pictures in the paper of Sophie than of Diana and Fergie put together. It was a very public four-day break on the Royal yacht Britannia.

There cannot be much argument that Sophie is very good at sport. She can ski, swim, scuba-dive, surf, play hockey and real tennis and all to a decent standard. On this particular break she decided to try her hand at windsurfing and water-skiing. It was a gift from heaven for the assembled photographers. In her mind Sophie saw a series of snaps showing her whizzing gracefully along the water in her striking black-and-red wetsuit. Instead she treated the Press to a sequence of daily pratfalls. First, she was water-skiing when her tow rope got tangled up in the propeller of a speedboat and she ended up stranded in the water. Princess Anne's son Peter Phillips dived in gallantly to try to free the rope, but in the end Sophie had to be rescued — by a passing dinghy full of photographers! Sophie was a bright shade of crimson as they took her good-naturedly to shore. Next came windsurfing and Sophie's 'game for a laugh' holiday gathered pace. While Edward patiently, if a little exasperatedly, looked on she tried her hand at windsurfing. She started well and then resumed her close acquaintance with the Solent. Pictures of her humiliation were 'splashed' all over the newspapers. It was the first and last time she has been pictured having such 'fun'. When a reporter harmlessly asked her if she was enjoying herself she snapped his head off and replied: 'We are not!' Sophie does have a rather tetchy side to her nature, which she usually keeps hidden, but it can rise to the surface if her patience is stretched. And making a fool of herself for the benefit of millions of newspaper readers stretched it. It can only be a small coincidence that she and Edward danced at the Royal Yacht Squadron Ball to strains of 'I Will Survive' by Gloria Gaynor. It has become increasingly clear that this is a perfect signature tune for Miss Sophie Rhys-Jones.

Around this time there surfaced a totally false story in Australia that seemed designed to undermine Sophie and Edward's relationship. If it had become public over here, it might well have proved a scandal too far. It was the sort of Royal 'sexploit' that would have whipped Hollywood producers into a frenzy. Charismatic Australian test all-rounder Greg Matthews said he had been offered more than half a million Australian dollars (£250,000) to confess that he had been Sophie's lover. Greg said he was one of several Aussie test stars who had been targeted over a six-month period as the mystery cricketer with whom Sophie was alleged to have had an affair. Fleet Street newspapers were in a lather of excitement over the rumours, which had been mysteriously leaked from Royal sources. Greg recalls: 'I thought they were trying to use me to destroy Sophie. The whole episode caused my wife Jill and me great anguish. She was very upset when London newspapers started ringing asking about my so-called relationship with Sophie. I thought "My God, what have we done to deserve this?" I must admit you get extremely paranoid even though you're totally innocent. I found the whole thing very sinister — there must have been some people out there trying to create problems.' Every time one of them picked up the phone the price would go up until it eventually reached 550,000 dollars. Eventually after the tenth call, Greg discovered the affair was supposed to have happened during the 1993 Ashes tour, a trip he was not even on. It transpired that all that happened was that during the tour Sophie had joined the Wallaby cricketers at a pub quiz night called the 'Aussie Brain Strain', sponsored by Castlemaine XXXX. Greg was not the only one given a grilling, but he seems to have been politer than most. When a reporter from the *Sun* went to the home of all-rounder Steve Waugh, he was told by the cricketer's wife to 'XXXX off'. In the end nothing appeared in the newspapers, although Fleet Street, like an elephant, never forgets a possible story.

Sophie's next ordeal by 'media' came in October 1995 at the hands, of all people, *Hello!* magazine. This bible of the bland is such a toothless creature that it seems hard to believe the magazine caused Sophie so many sleepless nights that she eventually sought the advice and reassurance of the Queen herself. *Hello!* has peddled so many pictures of Diana and, especially, Fergie that it was only a matter of time before Sophie was put under the spotlight. The means by which this was achieved was a triumph of canny journalism. It also proved to be the final nail in the coffin of her job in front-line PR. An independent company put together a package for *Hello!* to produce an issue centred around a charity launch for Baby Lifeline, a cause that Sophie is particularly devoted to and not just in her capacity as a PR executive. The idea was that *Hello!* would produce £25,000 worth of sponsorship for Baby Lifeline, which was certainly not to be sneezed at. *Hello!* would sponsor a dinner that would give them access to Sophie and Edward. The whole shebang was presented to Sophie as a *fait accompli*. She had, to quote a friend who does not wish to upset *Hello!*, been 'put into a corner'.

So what was Sophie to do? If she pulled out, Baby Lifeline would not get the £25,000 and she would be letting down a lot of people. Sophie felt she was being railroaded into giving what amounted to a personal interview — something that she would normally never countenance. Sophie does not give interviews. She had a private audience with the Queen where she was at pains to point out that, unlike the Duchess of York, she was not trying to capitalise in any way on her position as a Royal girlfriend. The Queen was not too bothered. If Sophie had announced she had been pregnant, the Sovereign's eyebrow might have been raised a notch, but the Queen regarded it all as part of growing up.

In the end Sophie handled the event brilliantly. She personally contacted the Marquesa de Varela, the magazine's chief international fixer and put her foot down about copy and picture approval. She insisted that the focus of the feature be Baby Lifeline and not Sophie Rhys-Jones. Not for the first time Sophie gritted her teeth and refused to let things get the better of her. The event was held at Weston Park, the Shropshire stately home owned by the Earl of Bradford, who is better known as the founder of Porters restaurant in Covent Garden. It was a sparkling success and Sophie showed new self-assurance reflected in her choice of dress for the occasion — she wore a bottle-green velvet gown that swept to the floor and four strands of pearls around her neck. Luckily it was not a cool evening as the frock plunged both front and back, which could have meant an evening of goosebumps.

Sophie chatted happily with guests, many of whom, including Chris Tarrant and Paul Daniels, seemed to be clients of Brian MacLaurin who turned up in a kilt. Robert Powell and his wife Babs were there to help make Sophie feel at ease — after all, she was on show. It was a fantastic evening. Even Edward enjoyed it. The first guest speaker was Rory Bremner, the award-winning impersonator, who failed to address Edward as Your Royal Highness at the start of his speech. When he had finished, Chris Tarrant, who is well known to enjoy some liquid refreshment, stood up and announced, 'Rory, you cannot be forgiven. You are in the presence of King Edward. He's bound to be the next king because the others aren't going to make it.' Edward's foghorn laugh echoed around Weston Park.

Afterwards Sophie had an anxious two-week wait before the *Hello!* exclusive appeared. *Hello!*'s Spanish owner Eduardo Sanchez Junco had brought all his family over from Spain for the event, so Sophie was quietly hopeful that the magazine would do its best for her. She has never looked lovelier than she does in those pictures. Certainly her teeth have never looked whiter, especially in the broad smile she displayed on the front cover. They matched her pearls. The banner headline announced THEY DANCED ALONG WITH 200 GUESTS — SOPHIE RHYS-JONES AT THE AUTUMN BALL HELD IN WESTON PARK IN AID OF BABY LIFELINE. It also slipped in PORTRAIT OF THE WOMAN WHO HAS CAPTURED THE PRINCE'S HEART. Inside, eleven pages were basically devoted to Sophie. She was pictured chatting to Edward, dancing with him to the sounds of the Pasadena Roof Orchestra, talking to Chris Tarrant, tripping lightly across the floor with someone called Frederick Nolan and enjoying the company of actor Ben Kingsley, a patron of the charity. And all the time Sophie's smile shone like a beacon.

Baby Lifeline founder Judy Ledger has always been fiercely diplomatic where Sophie is concerned. 'Sophie's support and encouragement have been astounding,' cooed Judy. Sophie had agreed to talk to

Hello! about the charity at her office in Hammersmith a few days before the ball. Judy was there and all the questions were about the charity, which was a pity as everyone was far more interested in whether Edward had smelly socks or whether he left the top of the loo seat up after having a pee. But it was the nearest anyone has ever got to an interview with Sophie and *Hello!* are to be congratulated for that. The article finished with a page of potted biography that gave no insight at all into the real Sophie Rhys-Jones.

Perhaps, in retrospect, the most noteworthy point about that evening, which everyone agrees was a great triumph for Sophie, was the support of Edward even if he was the last guest to turn up. The entire event was exclusive to *Hello!* so there were no paparazzi lurking in the bushes for Edward to worry about, but in all honesty he allowed the public to see what a changed man he has become since his relationship with Sophie has blossomed into love. They made a glamorous couple and he was confident and relaxed, a picture he was able to cement later with his first television documentary on his great uncle, the Duke of Windsor. He had stood by Sophie during one of the biggest evenings of her life. The only worry the two of them had was whether the curse of *Hello!* would strike them. This is the alarming coincidence, often pointed out with glee in the national Press, of how often couples featured in *Hello!* split up.

One of the happier spin-offs from the *Hello!* evening is that Sophie has struck up a friendship with the Marquesa and the two women have been seen dining together in London. Sophie feels she can trust the Marquesa who has always been the public face of *Hello!* She is a strong and exotic woman and for 14 years has had a magic key to the front doors of the rich, famous and beautiful who have invited *Hello!* on to their luxurious sofas and into their glistening blue swimming-pools while the rest of the world's Press cannot get past the wrought-iron gates at the end of drive. Sophie is fascinated by this woman who began life an undisclosed number of years ago as the daughter of a wealthy Uruguayan cattleman. She was married to a Spanish aristocrat, the Marques de Varela, and it is a tribute to her celebrity that she is instantly recognisable by just her title alone. If Prince Edward for instance was referred to merely as 'Prince' everyone would safely assume the subject of the conversation was a black Labrador. It is ironic that the Marquesa should eventually come under the media spotlight not in the anaemic *Hello!* style, but because of an almighty row between her and the magazine's editor Maggie Koumi. The Marquesa has a collection of *bon mots* of which Zsa Zsa Gabor would be proud and Sophie finds very entertaining. She particularly enjoys her view of the male sex. 'The more I know about men, the more I love my dog' is embroidered on her pillow. She was outraged when the perennial gossip columnist Nigel Dempster described her as the lady with the Louis Vuitton suitcase full of money. 'I hate Vuitton,' she declared, 'they are for the *nouveau riche*. That's not me.'

Sophie might feel she can trust the Marquesa, but that proved not to be the case with a certain German lawyer whose revelations have been the most indiscreet so far about Sophie. The only good point about the *Sun* exclusive of MY NIGHT IN POTTING SHED WITH SOPHIE was that it appeared on the day that the front page was devoted to the DIVORCE TODAY of

Charles and Diana. The *Sun* had dug up a lawyer from Germany who revealed a naughty night he had spent at a party thrown by Sophie's flatmate Ulli. He recalled: 'It happened after a sweltering summer's day in 1992.' The party turned out to be the memorable one in the back garden of Ulli's stepfather's house in Benenden where, after some dancing and kissing, Sophie had adjourned to the shed with a handsome German student who was now a fully fledged lawyer. He revealed: 'I had my sleeping bag with me and I put it on the ground. Then Sophie and I started kissing ...' Thank heavens he stopped short of giving Sophie marks out of ten.

Meanwhile the *News of the World* had managed to drag up the film she had made as a favour to some friends a few months before she met Edward. FILM SHOCK FOR PRINCE ED. SHE DANCES IN TIGHT MINI. The copy was suitably breathless: 'In a skin-tight backless minidress Sophie gyrates wildly under the strobe lights to the rasping rap anthem 'White Lines'. Then the lusty-eyed beauty wraps herself round a handsome stranger for that lingering kiss.' And then ... That's it. Nothing happens. It is not exactly in the same league as Koo Stark who took her clothes off in *Emily* and had to suffer the indignity of being described *ad nauseum* as a soft porn star when she was going out with Prince Andrew. Koo always conducted herself with dignity and is a surprisingly good role model for Sophie. A Buckingham Palace servant recently said, 'All the staff thought the world of Koo and we were really disappointed when they split up. She was always very good to us, polite, and treated us like human beings. She was not nearly so demanding as the Duchess of York.' Sophie could do a lot worse than aspire to be similarly described.

Far from being a film 'shock' for Edward, Sophie's career as a budding Emma Thompson reduced him to tears of laughter. Although occasionally prone to the family arrogance, Edward is not a prude, has mixed enthusiastically with the acting profession and has always enjoyed treading the boards himself. Even Edward knows the difference between a screen kiss and 'Deep Throat'. It is unlikely that Sophie will continue her screen career, but it was a laugh. Somewhat aptly the film was entitled *Horizons*. Sophie's own horizons are considerably broader these days.

19

The Firm's Apprentice

Sophie told her Australian friend Eon Balmain during a telephone conversation when he was visiting London, 'I haven't gone through all this for nothing.' It was a light remark that revealed the inner steel of the woman who has managed to maintain a healthy relationship with a member of the Royal Family through a number of setbacks and disappointments. There are wonderful prizes attached to becoming a member of The Firm, but it is not an easy family to join. Sophie knew she would continue to be under constant scrutiny and one slip could mean the end of her dream. The Royal Firm has been wounded so badly that it now flinches at the slightest scratch. When Sophie first reached her 'understanding' with Edward in the New Year of 1994 she had not bargained on having to wait another five years for 'the calmer waters'. In effect, she has spent five years as an apprentice doing work experience as a Royal princess. She has been doing the job, but not getting the rewards a fully fledged company employee would enjoy.

Eon Balmain's enlightening phone conversation with Sophie — which he revealed to the *Sun* — left him in no doubt that she was determined not to 'blow' her relationship: 'She told me, "I've had to make certain sacrifices to reach this point and I haven't done it for nothing." It was almost as if her intentions were "I want to do it right and I want to do it right for Edward." She wants to be seen as a mature person with the attributes to handle moving into the Royal Family and with no skeletons in the cupboard. She said she had to be careful about what she says to people and be sure they didn't take it the wrong way. She said that everything she did or said was put under the microscope and she couldn't afford to put a foot wrong. I had the impression she was conscious of her new station in life. I felt she wanted to tell me something, but she couldn't. Obviously she was very excited and she said things were moving quickly. She's very determined not to let go of Edward, that came across pretty loudly. She sounded as if her mind was already made up and this was it. Edward was her prize. There's no way he would be dumping her and she's not about to dump him. She also made it clear she was expecting a bit of privacy and trust from her friends.'

That last sentiment proved to be particularly appropriate where Eon was concerned because, although she did not know it at the time, he would return to haunt Sophie with the sort of news that she had been dreading. But that was a year away and in the meantime Sophie was happy to chat to him as an old holiday friend and to be very straightforward about her life, especially in revealing that things were moving quickly. That was certainly the case back in November 1995 when everything seemed to be moving rapidly to a perfect conclusion for Sophie. She should have realised that nothing is ever resolved simply where the Royal Family is concerned.

In the wake of the *Hello!* feature on Baby Lifeline, Edward, prompted by the Palace machine, had suggested that she should give up being a front-line PR executive. Sophie, forever sensible, saw that she could not possibly be put into that position again, especially if she were a princess or a duchess. She was also desperate for money. She was finding it impossible to be a princess in all but name on less than £400 per week. It was with a great deal of regret that she handed in her notice to Brian MacLaurin on 22 November, two days after one of the most momentous events in the history of the Royal Family — Diana's *Panorama* interview. Sophie's willingness to bow to pressure from Edward to distance herself from bumping into the Press on a daily basis was a great plus in her favour. A girlfriend of Sophie's explained: 'Sophie reflects the company line at all times. If the company hated the Panorama programme, then Sophie hated it. She is very smart like that. She is very controlled about Press stories and never comments on any Press story about herself — not even the one about the German in the potting shed!'

Sophie had really enjoyed working at MCM and Brian had done a great deal to help her through the hazards of being a Royal girlfriend. A former friend and colleague Nick Skeens believes, 'Brian MacLaurin was brilliant for Sophie.' She loved the fast pace and the buzz of mixing with celebrity clients like Jimmy Nail, Noel Edmonds and Paul Daniels. She had always enjoyed that ever since her days at Capital Radio. During her month's notice, Sophie set about organising her future life so that everything would be settled in time for the engagement announcement. After all, this time it was actually going to happen. With Brian's agreement it was decided she would continue her association with Baby Lifeline, a cause so close to her heart, and the high-society caterers Searcy's. She would also work two days a week for the Duke of Edinburgh's Award Scheme helping with the organisation's newsletter. Major-General Michael Hobbs, its loyal chairman, insisted they thought of Sophie because of her experience and not because she was Edward's girlfriend. He added, 'If we commission her to do some work for us, she'll be paid like anybody else.' Sophie was also given the perk of a Rover Metro as a company car. The remainder of her working week would be spent as a PR consultant for a company called Hollander, off the beaten track in unfashionable South Acton on a slow road out of West London. She would guide and advise instead of being in the front line. Palace courtiers, who had never approved of Sophie being so close to journalists, were delighted and they went onto red alert for an engagement announcement. What could go wrong?

Edward did his bit to fuel the fire by nipping into Garrard's, the Royal jewellers, and looking at engagement rings. At first Edward had planned to go down on bended knee straight away but, after Diana's volcanic *Panorama* programme his natural caution got the better of him once again and he decided to wait until the fuss about that interview had died down. Sophie, who had become used to waiting, could only shrug her shoulders and tell her mother and father not to get the champagne out of the fridge just yet. Ever the actress, she was accomplished at hiding her disappointment. It was decided that they would make a New Year announcement and Edward suggested they hold an engagement party at Buckingham Palace for their closest friends. They decided on Thursday 11 January which would give everyone the chance to get back to London after Christmas and the New Year. They decided to keep the occasion small and intimate — no more than the size of a large dinner party. Edward's private dining-room is comfortable for about a dozen guests. If they had wanted something grander, it would have involved going through official channels to use one of the large main Palace rooms. That is not Edward's style. He wanted to let his trusted chums know his plans before he made a formal announcement to the world. He did, however, confide to a friend that he could picture himself walking with Sophie across the frost-covered lawns of Buckingham Palace displaying their love to the world.

Sophie and Edward's engagement party on 11 January went ahead and was a great success. Sophie was vivacious and happy and all their friends had a super evening. Only one ingredient was missing: the couple did not announce their engagement. In the space of one short month Sophie's dreams were again crushed by spectacular events elsewhere. The catalyst was just seven words spoken on the afternoon of 14 December at the Lanesborough Hotel where Charles and Diana held their joint Christmas party for their 70 servants and other staff. Diana edged up to Charles' rumbustious assistant Tiggy Legge-Bourke, and declared 'So sorry to hear about the baby.' Diana was making an oblique reference to a groundless story that had been doing the rounds of so-called Royal circles that autumn. Apparently, Diana was convinced that not only was her estranged husband having an affair with her children's nanny but that Tiggy had gone abroad for an abortion. It was a remark that left Tiggy understandably shocked and her wealthy family, who had a long tradition of Royal service, so incensed they issued a legal rebuttal through the well-known libel lawyer, Peter Carter-Ruck. Tiggy stopped short of actually suing Diana. When the Queen got to hear of it, she was furious.

The rest, as they say, is history. The Queen wrote to Diana and Charles with what in effect was a Sovereign's command to get divorced as soon as possible. The letter was leaked in a clever if predictable move thereby putting Diana into the impossible position of having to agree a divorce or be seen openly to defy the Queen. It also prevented Charles from being blamed for starting divorce proceedings. From that day on, her days as Her Royal Highness were numbered and the divorce deal was about what any wife of a very rich man might reasonably expect.

At this point Prince Edward put his foot down. 'The Queen Machine' of senior courtiers wanted to use his romance with Sophie to shield his brothers' divorce announcements but he was having none of their scheming.

The Yorks' divorce proved to be relatively easy. Diana's divorce was a more difficult proposition and the strategy was to leak the divorce details in dribs and drabs so that it appeared to be old news by the time it went through. Secretly everyone was hoping to announce it to coincide with a peace settlement in Northern Ireland, but when that did not happen the Palace settled on 12 July, the day Tony Blair announced the Labour party manifesto. Even the Queen raised a chuckle when a senior member of the family referred to the day as 'The Glorious 12th!' Royal expert Margaret Holder observed, 'It was a private victory for Edward. He had refused to be used. He had stood his ground and won.'

Sophie's joy that Edward's eldest brother had finally done the decent thing and obtained a divorce was somewhat tempered by a story the same day that she had enjoyed a night in a potting-shed with a German lawyer. No one, however, could take much interest in that piece of tittle-tattle and she was heartily relieved to sweep it under the carpet. She realised she would now become the centre of yet more fevered speculation about their engagement announcement. It seemed scarcely a week had ever gone by without that announcement being confidently predicted by someone. It would be at Christmas, then New Year, then her birthday, his birthday, Valentine's Day and so on. Only Edward knew. Sophie had to admit to friends that she did not have a clue, but would be ready when he was ready. Having agreed to be unofficially engaged for three years, she could hardly turn around and throw a wobbly now.

Some progress had been made, however. At the time of their 'engagement' party in January they had dinner with the vicar, in this case his old friend Tim Hastie-Smith, chaplain at Stowe School. Basically Tim told them not to be too hasty. 'They have had a difficult time, but they are being sensible and taking their time. They are playing their cards close to their chest,' he said afterwards. Sophie and Edward had now narrowed the venue for their wedding down to two possibilities. Sophie had her heart set on St George's Chapel at Windsor Castle, which she had adored ever since she had first nervously stayed at the great Royal home in late 1993. The other possibility was the parish church at Craithie, just outside the gates of Balmoral, where Edward's sister Anne had married her second husband Commander Tim Laurence in 1992. Both Sophie and Edward had loved their stays at Craigowan Lodge and the bracing walks across the Scottish moors. The couple are agreed on one point — they will get married with a minimum of fuss and pomp and ceremony. They are acutely aware, as is the Queen, at the huge amount of public money wasted on the weddings of Edward's brothers and sister. The priority for Edward will be to avoid hoards of paparazzi hanging from every vantage point trying to get *the* picture of the happy couple. For that reason alone they could never marry in Brenchley, although secretly Edward would like to be the normal chap rolling up to his bride's home church with his best man in the manner of *Four Weddings and a Funeral*, a film he greatly enjoyed.

As planned, Sophie had left MCM on 22 December. That was not before yet another company Christmas party was wrecked by the media. She had joined Brian MacLaurin and the other 16 members of staff for dinner at Deals Restaurant in Hammersmith, only for Brian to identify journalists from the *Sun* and the *Mirror* at nearby tables. And when the paparazzi burst in and rattled off machine-gun pictures of Sophie, the entire evening was ruined. Everyone just sat there hardly daring to move. If nothing else, Sophie was happy that she had made the right decision to move into more of a backwater. As ever, Brian MacLaurin was full of praise for his account manager when she left. 'I never know what a good PR person is or what a good PR person does but from the moment I met Sophie I knew she was a girl who could charm the birds out of the trees. Whenever a client met Sophie they would feel she was a girl who knew what she was up to.'

Her ex-colleague Leanne Tritton-Jones observed: 'Quite often Sophie was in a difficult position because her job was to talk to the Press all the time, but that never scared her off. She was very good at her job. There was never any screening of her calls like "Who are you? What do you want?" or anything like that. It didn't matter who you were, whether from a regional or a national newspaper, if you phoned up in connection with one of her accounts, she would just take the call.' Nick Skeens recalls how interesting it was to see Sophie cope with the inevitable line of questioning from journalists. 'They would phone about Baby Lifeline or some other charity or even Mr Blobby, which was an account we had. You just knew that the journalist at the end of the phone was waiting and at the end of the conversation was going to say "Oh, by the way, how is your relationship going? Are you going to get married?" At this point Sophie would put up the barriers and the journalist would have to back off. I would have lost my rag with the Press. I would have lost my rag with Buckingham Palace and I would have lost my rag with just about everybody and it would have been a disaster. But Sophie has this great ability to handle her situation.'

On the day Sophie left, Brian MacLaurin walked her to her car as he had done on the day all hell let loose after Andrew Morton had revealed her Royal romance to the world. She was bowled a few questions by waiting journalists about her Christmas plans and the possibility of an engagement, but dropped a safe bat on all of them. How Sophie had changed since she joined MacLaurin. She was no longer the casually dressed, tousle-haired girl back from Australia. All the rough edges had gone. There was literally not a hair out of place as she declared, 'I am just changing jobs,' and drove off in her N-registration Rover. It had all been very careful planned and Sophie had actually been reluctant to pander to the journalists, but she had been persuaded by photographer Andrew Murray who told her 'Come on. It's your last day.' Andrew had been in earlier for a chat with Brian MacLaurin about the best way to handle things because they both knew the Press would turn up and they also realised the importance of a last picture of her leaving. They decided Sophie should come out with a large bunch of flowers and that Brian would escort her to her car and give her a farewell kiss. Despite Sophie's misgivings, she handled it all brilliantly as usual and everyone was happy.

Her apprenticeship to The Firm acted like sandpaper on her personality. One of her close friends confided that her greatest fear for Sophie is that she is becoming bland, 'She has had to be on her guard so much, about what she says and does that it's now become natural for her.' Nick Skeens agrees, 'When I first met Sophie she was very open and jolly. She has definitely become more introspective, always concerned and aware that tittle-tattle from the office could end up in the tabloid Press and create the sort of publicity she would not welcome. I don't know how the Palace treated her, but I imagine she would have been briefed fairly thoroughly on the sort of stories that were likely to create problems for Edward or the Royal Family.'

One such story, of course, would have been a kiss and tell. That nearly happened in the summer when the name of Eon Balmain became of interest again to Fleet Street newspapers. Insiders on the Sunday tabloids say he was offered in the region of £5,000 for what he knew, but that he was assured that he could add a nought to that if he was going to say Sophie and he had enjoyed a sexual relationship. The papers were desperate to find someone who would admit to sleeping with Sophie and at that time Eon Balmain seemed the best option. In the end all that was revealed was the old potting shed story and everyone could draw breath. In this instance Eon Balmain would not follow suit and change his original story to say he had made love to Sophie and the entire business went cold.

In the meantime Sophie was much more upset by the adverse publicity in August about her pet charity Baby Lifeline than about the 'sensational' revelation that she had shared a German lawyer's sleeping bag. The *Daily Mirror* exclusively revealed that Baby Lifeline had spent nearly 85 per cent of its income on administration. The charity had raised £635,000 in three years, thanks in some measure to the reflected Royal patronage that Sophie brings as PR consultant, but an embarrassing total of just £105,000 had been given to hospitals. The story sent the children's charity on a fast track to financial ruin because it practically wiped out contributions overnight. It was not Sophie's fault in any shape or form and she immediately threw all her energy into supporting the charity, but the adverse publicity was another weapon for all those who advocate her withdrawal from anything remotely public. It was a bitter blow to Sophie who kept Baby Lifeline as a client when she left Brian MacLaurin's agency and was doing her best for the charity. Her official title was National Events and Projects Organiser and in that role in March she organised a fashion show for toddlers to mark Mother and Baby Week. She roped in close friend Chris Tarrant for a champagne reception at the Mayfair Hotel in London. Then there was the social triumph of the *Hello!* ball for Baby Lifeline. In view of Fergie's appalling financial track record, the last thing the Royals wanted was another controversy to do with money. As a Palace source said during the revelations over the debts of the Duchess of York, 'Where will it all end? We'll be finding out next that the Queen Mother has had an overdraft for years. We don't want the public to know anything about Royal affairs. The divorce settlement between the Prince and Princess of Wales put a most unwelcome spotlight on Royal fortunes.'

Fortunately the Charity Commissioners gave Baby Lifeline a clean bill of health having discovered that the problem had been an accountancy error and Sophie was reassured that nothing irregular had taken place. Sophie put on her best PR hat and issued a brief statement that could have come out of the mouth of a Westminster politician. She said: 'I am delighted that everyone who has worked so hard to make a success of the charity can now get on with the task of raising money for maternal services and special-care baby units.' The storm in the balance sheet was more accurately described by Sophie's friend Judy Ledger, the charity's founder. She groaned: 'It has been an absolute nightmare and financially devastating. It's a tremendous relief to be exonerated. Sophie has been so supportive. It's an honour to have her working with us.' Judy's last remark reflects the change in the perception of Sophie. She is no longer a PR executive — to all intents and purposes she is a Royal. It is always an honour to work with a Royal, never a pleasure. It turned out to be an honour that Baby Lifeline was not going to enjoy much longer. Within a couple of months of the news first hitting the newspapers, Sophie withdrew.

Edward and Sophie had both turned 30 and were in danger of becoming the only unmarried couple they knew. They were always turning up as guests at someone else's wedding. And their presence always attracted the most attention — Edward in tails and Sophie in a new frock and an unfortunate hat.

As long ago as April 1994 they were the high-profile guests at the wedding of two of their best friends, Lord Ivar Mountbatten and Penny Thompson. Everyone was convinced it was just a rehearsal for their own wedding. A crowd of 800 people, which had gathered outside the parish church of Clare in rural Suffolk, burst into spontaneous applause when they realised Edward had brought Sophie to what was very nearly a Royal wedding. As far as the Queen is concerned, the Mountbattens are very much part of the family. Lord Ivar's great uncle Earl Mountbatten, or 'Uncle Dickie' as Prince Charles always called him, was murdered by the IRA in 1979, a black day for the Royal Family and a true outrage.

Sophie wore a split black skirt and a red jacket to the wedding and sat next to Princess Margaret in the back of a limousine while Edward sat in front next to his bodyguard Brian. As usual Sophie walked two steps behind Edward who gave no outward sign of affection towards her. That is the Royal Family's way and has no bearing on how the couple behave in private. Like the rest of his family Edward is not a 'touchy' type of person and observers have looked in vain for any physical chemistry between him and Sophie, at least in public.

There seemed to be a wedding every Saturday during the summer of 1994. In May Sophie left Edward behind at the Royal Windsor Horse Show to go to Fulford near York for the wedding of her friend Geraldine Turner to London chef Mat Williams. On the way home she was laughing and joking with friends when the Volkswagen Golf they were travelling in was involved in a bad shunt and was written off. A shaken Sophie and her pals had to hitch up their wedding outfits and get a lift in a break-down truck. A week later Sophie donned a large broad-brimmed black hat and Edward wore tails when his friend Clair Parker married Jeremy Fisher at the village of Faulbourne in Essex. It poured with rain, which gave the newspaper headline writers a chance to exercise their creative juices. POUR BETTER OR WORSE ... SOPHIE IS A SPLASHER was the best of a damp bunch.

Three months later Sophie wore a disastrous drum

majorette outfit to the wedding of Lady Sarah Armstrong-Jones to Daniel Chatto and Edward wore tails. It was just the sort of low-key affair that Sophie and Edward want for themselves, although presumably Sophie is hoping that on her own wedding day she will not have to walk two paces behind her husband. In December Sophie wore a black skirt, gold top and an ill-judged black hat while Edward wore tails to the wedding of two other great friends Anastasia Cooke and James Baker, son of Richard Baker.

Perhaps the most poignant reminder to Sophie that everyone is beating her to the altar was the wedding last September of her brother David. Sophie has always had a soft spot for her brother who is a very sociable and popular fellow much at home in country society — he takes after his father in that respect. He has been shooting with Edward in Kent and at Sandringham. David has been working for an insurance company after losing his job with a frozen food company, but his great love is commentating at racecourse meetings. He is much in demand and takes control of the microphone at the Mid-Surrey Farmers Draghunt Point to Point at Charing where Sophie spent many a happy Saturday in her teens. Sophie tried hard not to take the spotlight away from him or his bride Zara Friedland but, needless to say, the scrum of photographers who gathered outside the parish church of Northiam, ten miles from Cranbrook, were interested only in Sophie and Edward. As the Prince left the church an elderly guest was knocked to the ground when the photographers surged forward. 'It's a rehearsal' was the cry of the day, which begs the question of just how many rehearsals Sophie and Edward need. It was, however, a happy day for Sophie's parents, who have been so supportive of her during her Royal romance. And, for the very first time,

Edward was pictured between his 'in-laws'.

Edward and Sophie were in danger of sinking into comfortable middle age. Privately, people were beginning to notice a change in Sophie. Capital Radio DJ Dr Fox confirmed that her friends had noticed a different demeanour. He acknowledged: 'The change, as we can all probably imagine, is that she is just exceedingly defensive. You get mates going out together and if anyone is going out with someone new you want to know all about him and what he's really like. That's particularly true if he's a prince. She's obviously paranoid about saying anything because she is very discreet.' Experienced photographers like Tim Graham also noticed that Sophie was beginning to turn away to avoid a picture. It was as if Edward had won that battle because when they started going out he would go to great lengths to avoid them being photographed together. At one memorable house party at Wood Farm, one of Sophie's favourite weekend retreats on the Sandringham Estate, all the guests played a game known as 'Hide the Sophie'. When everyone came out of the house to walk in the fields all the girls dressed up as Sophie in hats and scarves and they kept swapping walking partners so any watching paparazzi would have been hopelessly confused. It was a hoot then, but avoiding being photographed had become an everyday reflex for Sophie.

The best way to avoid it was to stay in and most nights that 's exactly what Edward and Sophie did. They liked to have a light supper and watch *EastEnders*. Sophie loves the programme and her favourite character is the feisty Bianca Butcher whose 'game for anything' personality reminds her of her younger days. There are not too many princes in Albert Square, although Edward's hair is thinning at such an alarming rate he will soon be able to pass for one of the Mitchell brothers.

Television always plays a surprisingly large part in the life of the Royal Family. It is so much easier to stay in and watch it when to slip out for a swift half of bitter would involve such a kerfuffle and, besides, there are no photographers hiding behind the sofa at home.

The Queen's favourites are *Coronation Street* (although she was sorry to see Bet Gilroy leave), repeats of *Dad's Army*, *Keeping Up Appearances* and *One Foot in the Grave*. The Queen Mum likes these as well as any soppy film — she still adores *Brief Encounter* and always has some Kleenex handy — and , of course, she never misses the racing. It is a great Royal joke that Prince Philip bears an uncanny resemblance in manner to Victor Meldrew, the character so brilliantly portrayed by Richard Wilson in *One Foot in the Grave*. For his part Philip can see no resemblance whatsoever. Philip's great passion, which he shares with Edward and Charles, is wildlife films. His favourite broadcaster is David Attenborough. The Duke also loves cricket. At Royal Ascot in June he dutifully doffs his top hat to the crowds as he travels up the course in the open landau with the Queen. Once safely away from prying eyes he makes his way to the back of the Royal Box and spends the afternoon happily watching the Test match. Princess Margaret favours a bottle of Famous Grouse and a James Bond film. After a few stiff measures she can be neither shaken nor stirred from her chair if she is watching *The Spy Who Loved Me* with Roger Moore or, heaven, Sean Connery in *From Russia With Love*. He is just 'too handsome'.

None of The Firm will admit to watching satirical programmes, especially *Spitting Image*. Sophie was actually delighted when her puppet appeared on the show. A few years ago Charles was asked by a journalist what he thought about a particular sketch in which he featured on *Spitting Image*. 'I never watch that rubbish,' he snapped. 'That's a shame,' replied the reporter, 'they had a brilliant bit about Michael Heseltine as well.' 'Oh yes,' laughed Charles, enthusiastically, 'I did see that. It was good, wasn't it?' Fergie loved her representation as a gushing Sloane and watches all the new wave of humorous programmes like *They Think It's All Over* and *Have I Got News For You*. Her favourite is undoubtedly *Blind Date*, which she never misses. If *It's a Royal Knock-Out* had not been such an abject failure then it would have only been a matter of time before Royal Blind Date came along. One Palace servant, now secure in the knowledge that the Duchess will not darken their door again, joked, 'You would have to be blind to date that woman.' Prince Andrew's staff used to tape programmes for him while he was away at sea, although his current desk job has given him more free time at home alone. He likes comedies and golf. The thing about Andrew is that in real life he thinks he is funnier than Jim Davidson and is forever telling witless jokes. This is probably because Jim Davidson is too highbrow for him. Andrew finds farting really funny. The beautiful Romy Adlington, then Prince Edward's girlfriend, once gave an insight into this when she met the Duke of York for the first time at Sandringham. Andrew and Fergie were laughing hysterically about farting in the bath. Andrew asked Romy: 'Don't you think they always smell worse in the bath?' Fortunately Edward was on hand gallantly to steer the conversation to a more suitable Royal topic — namely, duck shooting.

Sophie does get on very well with The Firm. She knows, for instance, that there is one programme that is never going to grace the screens of Buckingham Palace again and one that she would never dare watch —

Panorama is the televisual equivalent of smallpox as far as the Royal Family are concerned. Her ace in the hole is the fact that the Queen and, in particular, the Duke of Edinburgh are on her side. The Queen has spotted something in Sophie that just did not exist in Diana or Fergie. She has recognised an inner strength that is so essential for anyone hoping to make a lifetime commitment to The Firm. Sophie does not surround herself with 101 gurus, therapists and hangers-on. She has always been, and hopefully always will be, self-sufficient. The Queen has made it of paramount importance from now on that none of her sons or grandsons will marry weak women. Royal expert Margaret Holder explains: 'Both Diana and Fergie came from dysfunctional families that broke up in their childhood rendering them statistically liable to have problems in their own marriages. Sophie comes from a very stable background and, although not upper-class, has enough family respectability to carry her through.'

Prince Philip has always had an eye for a pretty face. Romy Adlington once declared that the Duke had patted her bottom as he showed her to her room. He particularly likes blonde, lively, sporty girls to brighten up the rather staid Royal gatherings. He is not particularly taken with a fashion plate, but prefers girls who are happiest in jeans and sweaters. Sophie fits the bill perfectly. It is also a case of 'like father, like son' because Edward, for all his associations in his professional life with lovely young actresses, prefers a girl who slips more easily into a Barbour than between satin sheets. Sophie clearly mucks in. She enjoys joining in the parlour games, like passing a bottle without using one's hands. Philip is always particularly keen to pass the bottle to Sophie. She is also a passable mimic and can do impressions of most of the family. Sophie has confided to a friend that she likes Charles but finds him a bit 'aloof'.

Her most poignant observation on the Royal Family, to the same friend, is that she thought Andrew was 'a lonely, lonely man who was deeply depressed by life'. Sophie had been very moved by Andrew's situation when he was going through such a bad time with his now ex-wife. She was distressed at seeing him just 'moping' around — this compassion does her great credit. Andrew has had to look on helplessly as the Press pursue Fergie like a pack of hounds closing in on a three-legged fox. Even Sophie who has pillow access to the secrets of the Royal Family was shocked by the revelations of bizarre psychic Madame Vasso who became Sarah Ferguson's confidante in a series of astonishingly indiscreet taped conversations in which, among other things, she confessed to making love to Texan Steve Wyatt when she was five months pregnant. It was at this point that she and Andrew stopped having a sexual relationship. He has even had to endure reading in print a spectacularly inane telephone conversation that he had with Vasso in which she urges him in uncertain English, 'Be strong and I will tell you things will change, but you have to be strong. You are really nice, handsome, good man. And you have everything any woman can want, always.' 'Poor Andrew' is a sentiment echoing around the country and it is one that Sophie shares wholeheartedly. From her own point of view the Vasso tapes have made it imperative that she chooses her friends wisely and never entertains any guru, oddball or colonic irrigationist.

20

A Girl in a Million

It was time for Sophie to take stock of her situation. If the cards had fallen more favourably she would already have been Princess Edward by the time she joined the Queen, her boyfriend and other members of the Royals for the annual 'church parade' at Sandringham in the New Year of 1997. Press and public interest in the lives of Prince Charles and Princess Diana showed no signs of abating. Edward had made it quite clear that he did not want Sophie perceived as the 'saviour' of the Royal Family and Sophie was 100 per cent behind him on this. 'It is so absurd that anyone should think the Royal Family should need saving,' she has said.

For the past few months, she and Edward had been keeping a deliberately lower profile than before but, typically, their failure to appear in public together was interpreted as a cooling of their romance. Once again Sophie had to face up to a national newspaper, the

Sunday Mirror, telling the world Edward was going to part from her. The day before the article appeared they had been riding in Windsor Great Park and then watched the Barbarians rugby team play Australia at Twickenham. This time she ignored the headlines completely. She realised that the longer she and Edward remained unmarried the more likely it was that stories like this would emerge. There was absolutely nothing she could do about it.

Edward's advice was for her to follow his lead and throw herself into her work. Sophie was impressed by the way the fortunes of his own company Ardent Productions, had improved with the signing of a £2 million American TV deal. She could do with some of that herself. Although things were steadily improving, money was still of great concern to Sophie. She had been earning something in the region of £25,000 a year as an accounts manager for MCM, which, although not a bad wage among the Sloane set who inhabit the lower reaches of Chelsea and Fulham, was hardly in the multi-millionairess league of the Princess of Wales. Since leaving that job Sophie had been expanding her 'behind-the-scenes' consultancies, which, while not exactly cashing in on her Royal connections, would be very small beer without them. She had doubled her earning power, but in Royal terms was still on the breadline. As one Palace insider observed, 'She is expected to live like a princess, but she hasn't got the wherewithal. Money has become very important.'

Sophie decided that when she returned to London she would not sit around waiting to become a princess. She wanted to make sure she was secure for life if the papers were ever proved right and she and Edward did split. She got together with fellow PR consultant Murray Harkin with whom she was already working at

Hollander, and they decided to set up their own company. They gave themselves six months to get up and running. Edward was very enthusiastic about her plans and, just to show that their future together was still very much in his thoughts, he suggested that 1997 would be a good year to try and find somewhere to live when they eventually married.

Sophie was elated. 1997 looked set to be a crucial year for her. It would be like spring cleaning her life. The first thing she decided to do was find a new flat. She was still living in Vereker Road with her flatmate Ulli. The press seemed to think she was shacked up with Edward at Buckingham Palace as a blissfully happy common-law wife but that wasn't the case. Edward has a two-bedroom apartment at the Palace. When she stayed over, Sophie occupied one and Edward the other. She had security clearance to come and go as she pleased but was careful not to abuse the privilege. Although their relationship had been a sexual one for several years now, they were careful not to be too demonstrative in front of trusted servants and friends. Sophie is a very warm, loving and tactile person. When she stayed over, Edward made sure he was back in his own room by 5.30am ready for his valet to bring his early-morning tea and biscuits at 6.00am. It was a routine Edward was anxious not to upset and Sophie was happy to respect that.

Weekends have always been easier, because Edward is more relaxed when they are out of London, providing he does not think there are photographers lurking in the bushes. One of Sophie's favourite anecdotes concerns the time at Windsor when Edward was sneaking into her bedroom for a bit of a cuddle. On the way he had to creep past the Queen's bedroom, but in his ardent anxiety he accidentally trod on one of his mother's corgis asleep outside her door. The poor dog started howling and barking and Edward, forsaking all thoughts of passion, retreated hastily back to his room.

Sophie didn't have to look very far afield to find a flat she liked. A girlfriend she had met doing charity work offered her a room in her luxury flat. It was just a mile down the road from Vereker Road in a building she had driven past a thousand times. Coleherne Court is a mansion block in Earl's Court and had already enjoyed a moment of fame because it had been home to the then Lady Diana Spencer when she became engaged to Prince Charles. Although Sophie had been happy at Vereker Road the new place offered her greater security, privacy and luxury. She jumped at the chance to move in. She agreed to pay rent of just over £4,000 a year for the privilege of keeping her independence.

Part of the process of starting her own company would be cultivating the image of a successful PR. She started attending blue chip fashion events and taking a keen interest in all things designer. Up until now that had firmly been the province of Princess Diana. She popped over to Paris to take in an event sponsored by Louis Vuitton and murmured admiring noises at the parade of classic luggage. She was more enthusiastic about suitcases now than she had been when Edward had picked one out for her birthday present soon after they started dating. Most significantly she herself was sporting a very expensive Louis Vuitton handbag. Sophie began to play the social game where it was Gucci and Hermes one week followed by Asprey and Estée Lauder the next. The world of élite label PR which covers everything from clothes to cosmetics and luxury hotels is a very small one. It was all a million miles away from Mr Blobby and Mobil Oil and Sophie was well aware that her face had to fit — even though her boyfriend was the Queen's youngest son.

She took steps to improve her own image. She was stung when *Tatler* magazine described her as dressing like a dowdy Saffy, the character portrayed by Julia Sawalha in the television comedy *Absolutely Fabulous*. She was used to being unfavourably compared to Princess Diana, but realised that the Princess of Wales was a one-off fashion icon and no one could match her. Although Sophie has always been modest about her own appearance she was determined to make the very best of the raw material. Sophie is a size 12 and has referred to her 'sturdy Welsh legs' which is very unfair on herself as she is far more petite in the flesh than she appears in photographs. Her friend Leanne Triton-Jones observed: 'One of the things that first shocked me is how small she is. She is very slim. All that "Welsh legs" stuff is a load of rubbish. She has got great legs and she is very slim. Thank goodness she has maintained a sense of humour about all the personal comments. They are quite wounding. If Sophie is stocky then God help the rest of us.'

Fashion writer and stylist Alison Jane Reid highlighted the problem facing Sophie at this time: 'Everything about her shouts frumpy. She wears outfits for a much older Jean Brodie type of woman. She should stick to simple, clean shapes, pastel shades and clothes that enhance her athletic frame — shift dresses would be good for her. Sophie is a blank canvas for a fashion designer and ripe for experiment.' Perhaps with this in mind, Sophie cannily hitched her star to an up-and-coming designer in the knowledge that they could do each other a lot of good. The designer in question was Thomas Starzewski who made the whimsical fur-trimmed wedding dress of Diana's sister-in-law Victoria Lockwood in 1989. They established an informal partnership where Sophie would advise on public relations at a time when the entrepreneurial designer was expanding into foreign markets like Hong Kong. Sophie would give him invaluable publicity every time she was seen in one of his creations. Just how much discount she gets is something they keep to themselves but it is an alliance that has met with Edward's approval.

The flamboyant Starzewski, whose name does not sit lightly on the tongue like Versace or Dior, is the thirty-something son of Polish immigrants and very down-to-earth about his job as a fashion designer: 'I have to make a woman look the best she can. I must highlight the good points and hide the bad.' Sophie is naturally very pretty and photogenic and immediately caused a stir when she arrived at a party at Asprey, the Bond Street jewellers, wearing a fabulous raspberry pink off-the-shoulder evening dress that would have cost at least £1,500 to buy. It afforded Starzewski maximum publicity. Photographer Jayne Fincher was worried that Sophie looked uncomfortable in the low cut gown and heavy make-up. She commented: 'She's not confident enough in her looks to get away with that sort of outfit.' Diana Hutchinson of the *Daily Mail* unkindly declared that Sophie's neckline had 'all the attraction of an unplanted window-box'. Sophie, however, was growing in confidence all the time and this dress proved a big turning point for her. It's amazing what a £1,500 frock can do for a girl!

In the following months, Sophie's networking began to pay off. She knew that the new company which she and Murray decided to call R-JH, standing for Rhys-Jones Harkin, had to have a roll of clients to attract more business. First to sign up was Sophie's hairdresser Andrew Collinge, who was based in Manchester but came to London regularly for appointments in Harrods. He was already well-known for appearing as a hair expert on the Richard Madeley and Judy Finnigan show *This Morning*. He had been responsible for giving Sophie a short, layered bob. Alison Jane Reid maintains, 'Sophie looked more appealing when her hair was shoulder length and blunt cut. Andrew Collinge is a first class hairdresser but his styles seem more High Street than *haute-couture*.'

Thomas Starzewski was on board, of course, and Sophie was introduced to Rumi Verjee, the managing director of Thomas Goode, the society china company patronised by the likes of Prince Charles and Elton John. He thought Sophie had the right credentials to organise parties and events for him — a contract worth in the region of £80,000 a year to R-JH. You didn't need to be a rocket scientist to realise that those 'right credentials' involved the fact that Sophie was a Princess In Waiting. It was absolutely inevitable that her royal connections would open doors.

It was a time for furious work, but she and Edward did manage to get away for a June break in St Tropez. They stayed in a luxury house in the hills above the resort and spent their days sailing. They both needed the break. Sophie and Murray had finally found premises suitable for a prestige PR firm. They were in South Audley Street, Mayfair, in the same building as photographer Terry O'Neill's studio. Moving in had been exhausting, and Sophie was hoping to slip out of the country unnoticed. No such luck. The photographers found them and pictures appeared in the papers of Edward and Sophie allegedly looking glum. They were nothing of the kind, of course, but that was par for the course for the couple. They never smiled and waved for the benefit of the cameras so it was too easily assumed they were miserable.

Back home, Sophie excitedly prepared to tell the world about R-JH. The company was taken on by the Haven Trust breast cancer charity for a fee reported to be in the region of £60,000 a year. Sophie's brief was to put the charity on the map. She, having developed an acute business sense, immediately saw the perfect opportunity to promote the charity and R-JH. It would be in the pages of *Hello!* of course. She was interviewed and photographed over 12 pages of the society glossy. Sophie, fit and healthy after her holiday had never looked more radiant. She was pictured in her smart new offices. 'She's very proud of the beautiful table and she chose the prints on the wall herself,' cooed *Hello!*

Sophie has always had to tread a very careful line between courting the media in her work and avoiding them in her private life. In all the time she has been in the public eye as Edward's girlfriend this is the only full scale interview she has ever given. She seized the opportunity to inform the reader that her company was up and running with six employees. She was determined 'that people will seek out R-JH, not for her name but for the fact that the company delivers excellent results.' This had the ring of familiarity about it for those who had followed the career of Edward Windsor, always protesting his desire not to use his Royal name. The whole exercise was like a giant glossy brochure for R-JH, publicity which was liquid gold for a new company. The only scrap of insider knowledge about her relationship she provided for writer Sarah Cartledge was when asked what she and Edward had in common: 'We laugh a lot with each other and we have a number of interests in common. I love sport like he does but I am not always good at it. I learnt to windsurf but badly. My father had taught me how to sail but I never realised that the principle of windsurfing was the same as being in a boat. The penny dropped when Edward was instructing me one day. I yelled: "Now I understand!" and promptly fell back into the water.

'I don't profess to be a good rider because I'm not. I've got what is known as an electric bottom — whenever I sit on a horse it takes off, whether I want it to or not, always to everybody's amusement.'

The most revealing thing about those few modest remarks was that they clearly showed one of the principle reasons why Sophie had been accepted by the Queen and Prince Philip. She was happy to muck in and have a go. She was a trier.

Everyone was delighted with the *Hello!* piece. Sophie and Edward had joined the rest of the Royal Family on the traditional Western Isles cruise aboard *Britannia* which always preceded their summer holiday at Balmoral. Even Edward, who never liked press coverage of any kind, conceded that it was a superb article. He was secretly proud of how gorgeous his girlfriend looked. Everything looked very rosy indeed although they were still house-hunting. Even the stormy waters surrounding Charles and Diana were calming down. In that very same issue of *Hello!* Diana was photographed on holiday with new companion Dodi Fayed. They were pictured happy and relaxed on a five day cruise around the Mediterranean. Just two weeks later on 31 August Diana was dead. Her death affected the world like an atomic bomb of grief and the Royal Family took most of the fall-out.

There was nothing Sophie could do except slip even more into the background. She took what seemed a surprising decision not to attend Diana's state funeral. At the time it seemed a strange move but Sophie had chosen to stay at home for the best reasons of sensitivity. A friend at the Palace explained: 'Sophie decided it would be too upsetting for the crowd if she went. She's well aware that she looks like Princess Diana from a distance and made her decision in a caring and thoughtful way. The Royal Family fully supported that.'

All the Royal Family could do was keep their heads down and continue working and wait for the public to forgive and forget. Sophie had grown up a lot these past few years and quickly realised that there could be no marriage for a considerable time. It would not be fitting. Instead, Edward and Sophie hurled themselves back into work pausing only to consider possible houses. They were impressed with the handsome Newton Park, set in a handy four hundred acres on the edge of the New Forest in Hampshire. The asking price for the Palladian mansion was a cool £2 million. It was the setting for *The Music Lovers*, Ken Russell's erotic and controversial film about Tchaikovsky. There were six bedrooms, five reception rooms and an outdoor swimming pool which caught Sophie's eye.

Another likely candidate was Anmer Hall a large Georgian mansion on the Sandringham Estate. It had already served as a Royal home when it was leased by the Duke and Duchess of Kent. In the best Royal traditions there were no bathrooms en suite and the house was reputed to have a resident population of ghosts. One of these is said to be of the notorious Victorian financier E H Hooley who sold it to King Edward VII just before being jailed for three years for embezzlement. Sophie was not too keen on the prospect of being left alone in a home with just the ghost of E H Hooley for company.

In the end neither of these two splendid houses passed the most important test for Edward and Sophie.

Their future marital home had to be within one hour's drive of Buckingham Palace and Sophie's Mayfair offices. Eventually, thumbing through Crown Estate properties, they came across the magnificent Victorian gothic mansion Bagshot Park just a few miles down the road from Windsor Castle and conveniently close to the M25. The house had been built in 1877 on Queen Victoria's instructions as a wedding present for her third and favourite son, Prince Arthur, Duke of Connaught and Princess Louise Marguerite. They had married at St George's Chapel, Windsor, a portent perhaps of events to come. Edward drove Sophie out to take a look one weekend and she fell in love with it immediately. She told friends it had so much character. As anyone with experience of properties with 'character' will tell you, that description always means they need a lot of work. And Bagshot Park was no exception. Edward, having noted approvingly that the house was 'incredibly private' threw himself into plans and designs to restore the house to its former glory. It would be a challenge to relish.

Edward took a 50-year lease on the property from the Crown Estate — effectively making his mother his landlady — which would cost about £50,000 a year. The renovations which Edward wanted to restore the original character of the house would cost some £2 million. It was a grand project but one which the commercially astute Prince was keen to approach as a business strategy. When news of his purchase reached the media he told Colin Randall of the *Telegraph* that the cost of the work would be split between an off-the-shelf company created for the purpose of the project and the Crown Estate. To make it more cost effective he decided to move the whole of his Ardent Productions office into the stable block.

Sophie was happy to go along with the plans although she realised it would be well over a year before she would be choosing curtain material. She knew Edward was a perfectionist. He observed: 'It will require imagination and that little bit of extra effort. There is no point in just diving in and giving it an extra coat of paint.'

Bagshot Park, surrounded by trees, is set in 88 secluded acres of Crown Estates land. It has many wonderful features including its Portland stone and red brick Gothic façade and splendid wrought iron gates. Inside there is a chimney piece designed by Lutyens and an Indian room which was a wedding present to the Duke of Connaught from an Indian princess. The Duke died in 1942 at the ripe old age of 92 and the house became a wing of the Military Staff College at Camberley. After the War it was briefly considered as a country home for the young Princess Elizabeth before she became Queen. Instead it was made available to the Ministry of Defence and until 1996 was a training centre for Army chaplains when spending cuts forced its closure — luckily for Sophie and Edward.

The plans for the house were ironically to make it smaller, not bigger. The couple realised they would need to make it a more manageable size. There were just too many rooms. After all, the Duke of Connaught had more than 60 servants. Edward and Sophie planned to have just three members of staff living there: a chef, a secretary and Edward's trusted valet Brian Osborne. When everything was finished there would be nine ensuite bedrooms, five reception rooms and three staff flats. One complete wing would be demolished, but a private chapel would remain. Close to the house is a lake which quickly became a favourite haven of relaxation for Sophie on visits down to inspect the building work. Edward, displaying his trusty *It's A Knockout* humour, put up a sign which read 'Please don't walk on the water!'

On a more serious note, Edward stressed to Colin Randall that his plans for Bagshot Park and his relationship with Sophie were unconnected. He said: 'I have enough on my plate. They are totally separate issues. Obviously, if that changes, no doubt I shall have to tell people. But, however, please do not read too much into this in terms of any changes in my private life — certainly not at this stage for all sorts of reasons. This is not some circuitous route of changing my private life. These things will be announced when the time comes not before.'

Sophie and Edward's intention to marry had not wavered. Work on the house would take up to two years and there was no way of predicting when the nation, still pre-occupied with Diana's memory, would be ready for another Royal marriage. Edward was merely trying to pre-empt the inevitable speculation that the house would trigger.

The first priority was getting Ardent moved in. Edward would then be on the premises to oversee work on the main house. The summer of 1998 was pencilled in for the first stage of the work to be completed. In the meantime Edward's company made a number of successful royal based programmes and put into production a series of major costume dramas based on the popular Inspector Pitt novels written by Anne Perry. Edward had high hopes for the series. Ardent had lost £1.5 million since it began four years before, but the tide had turned and 1998 marked the start of profitability based on a turn-over of more than £3 million.

Sophie was doing even better. By May 1998 the annual income of R-JH was being estimated at close on a million. Sophie's share-holding was a very healthy 54 per cent. Her list of clients was the envy of the bitchy PR world, especially as she had only been open for business a year or so. Her blue-chip accounts included The Lanesborough Hotel, society jewellers Boodle and Dunthorne and Lady Apsley's School for Butlers. Trendy new gym, The Club at County Hall were quick to snap her up for £70,000. Her 17-page prospectus listed 16 similar clients. A huge breakthrough came when she landed the Comite Colbert account, the association for the French luxury goods trade. It was only worth £3,000, but in terms of PR prestige was priceless. Among the 75 association members were brands like Moet et Chandon, Chanel, Dior, Mercier, Wonderbra, Hermes and Christian Lacroix. These companies are big spenders. It was heady stuff for a girl not yet breaking the £20,000 barrier when she met Edward. Now she was earning ten times that and well on her way to her first million.

21

'Yes, Please!'

Edward finally moved Ardent Productions into Bagshot Park in August 1998, a month or two later than he had hoped. There was still so much work to be done that it would be well into 1999 before the main house was finished. While the couple waited for their own house to be ready so they could play host to their friends — something Sophie was longing for — they continued to enjoy country weekends staying with friends including the Bakers and the Mountbattens. They also spent weekends with former Warwickshire county cricketer Jonathan Howell, sports master at the Oratory School in Pangbourne, Berkshire. He and his Australian wife have three small children whom Sophie adores. They have a four-bedroom house in the school grounds, which makes a pleasant change from the vast country homes where Edward and Sophie usually spend their weekends. Edward has even been known to do the washing-up!

During the week they worked hard like any successful and ambitious couple, trying to keep out of the spotlight. Throughout 1998 the Royal Family gradually re-established itself as a popular institution. Much of the credit for that must go to the young princes William and Harry, who conducted themselves superbly in the months following their mother's death and were subsequently ready with a winning smile for the cameras. The obvious public affection for them did wonders for their father who was like a butterfly coming out of hibernation. It seemed that Charles was a new man, cheerful and caring and ready to be a sport as his various dealings with the Spice Girls revealed. His 50th birthday celebrations were greeted with genuine enthusiasm. Behind the scenes, Sophie helped organise his party at Highgrove. On the afternoon of the party she could be spotted in Tetbury doing some last minute shopping. Sophie was now so adept at slipping about unnoticed that you would have been forgiven for not knowing she was at the party. All the attention seemed to be on the 'celebrities' like Geri Halliwell. That suited Sophie perfectly.

In many ways she and Edward are a cosy married couple already, and she put any thoughts of her future wedding day (whenever that might be) to the back of her mind. Edward had mellowed considerably under Sophie's influence and they enjoyed a pleasant life sharing pursuits like riding and shooting among their close and loyal friends. Sophie has even had shooting lessons at Sandringham so that she can be upgraded from a beater and join in. The only slight cloud on the horizon was the thought that she would be celebrating her 34th birthday in January 1999 and her biological clock was ticking. Sophie has said that she wants children at some stage but would 'cross that bridge when she comes to it.' Edward will make a very good father. As long ago as 1993 when she was with him in Africa Jayne Fincher observed: 'He was very natural with the local kids. I think he sees the funny side in things and children like that.' This perhaps gives a clue as to why Sophie and Edward are so well matched. Yes, they have similar tastes and hobbies, but Sophie is a strong woman who understands Edward's sensitive nature, his generous spirit and innocent enthusiasm.

Just before Christmas, Edward impulsively whisked Sophie off for a three-day break to a romantic hideaway in Bermuda. He booked three nights at the £500 a night Pink Beach cottage colony, a paradise destination for couples with romance on their mind and one particularly popular with honeymoon couples. It's five miles from the capital Hamilton, and guests have a choice of two exclusive pink sand beaches to top up their tans while the Atlantic waves lap against the shore. After two idyllic sun-kissed days they were enjoying a candle-lit dinner when, to Sophie's amazement, Edward dropped to one knee and asked, 'Darling, will you marry me?' A stunned Sophie could barely speak the word 'yes' before finding her voice and replying , 'Yes, please!' Even though they had shared an understanding for several years, and had talked of marriage and planned their engagement announcement on many occasions, Edward had managed to take Sophie completely by surprise. They hadn't talked of it seriously for three years when Sophie's hopes had last been cruelly dashed. Edward's gallant proposal was a dream come true.

They flew back to England on 23 December and parted for Christmas at home with their respective parents. Sophie went to Brenchley and Edward to Sandringham. They promised to keep their wonderful news secret for a few days more so that Edward could formally ask Sophie's father for her hand. After a Christmas where poor Sophie was beside herself with anticipation and excitement they agreed that the world should share their news on 6 January. Sophie, who enjoys close informal links with royal jewellers Asprey & Garrard through her work, already knew the design of the engagement ring she wanted and Edward was happy to oblige. The jewellers promised it would be ready to sparkle before the world in the garden of St James's Palace. The Queen was delighted and a happy Sophie called Thomas Starzewski to talk about what she should wear for the big announcement. Edward who loves surprises was looking forward to springing this one on his friends in the media.

Unfortunately the high drama was slightly spoiled by *The Sun* who broke the news with a front-page story on the very morning of the announcement: EDWARD TO WED SOPHIE it boldly declared on its front page. The news rocketed around the world, not least to the pack of royal reporters and photographers who were completely taken by surprise on their annual skiing jaunt to Klosters trailing Prince Charles and his son Harry. The interest around the world was instant and phenomenal. At 10am, Buckingham Palace made it official. The announcement said:

> *The Queen and the Duke of Edinburgh are delighted to announce the engagement of their youngest son, Prince Edward to Miss Sophie Rhys-Jones. The couple sought the permission of their respective parents between Christmas and the New Year. Both families were thrilled at the news. No decision has been taken yet regarding the venue. However, Prince Edward and Miss Rhys-Jones hope*

that it might be possible to use St George's Chapel,
Windsor in the late spring or summer.

The whole world seemed to be thrilled. Certainly the
villagers of Brenchley were happy to send the couple
their best wishes. Sophie's father Christopher, a little
nervously told the press who gathered at his door, 'We
like Edward immensely and, of course, we have known
him for some time. He is a very, very nice chap. I think
Sophie will do very well. She has not exactly been
catapulted in — it's been a fairly long apprenticeship.' It
remains to be seen if he really will have to hock the
family silver to pay for the wedding as he has always
joked. Sophie's mother Mary was overjoyed and simply
said, 'I'm very happy,' her face a picture of smiles.

Shortly after the official announcement, Edward and
Sophie strolled out into the January sunshine to pose for
photographs in front of St James's Palace. She had
chosen to wear an hour-glass tailored suit with beaded
lapels and elongated silver buttons. It was a Starzewski
design and fittingly, considering the fashionable circles
Sophie now moved in, it was in the season's favourite
colour, grey. They were holding hands and smiling
happily. Her smile dazzled almost as much as her
fabulous diamond engagement ring. It was an
exceptionally pretty modern design of a triple white
diamond in a white gold setting. It oozed class, not
surprisingly considering the cost was variously
estimated at anywhere between £50,000 and £100,000.
The correct figure is £55,000. Edward, always keen to
impress with his quick wit, warned photographers, 'If it
catches the sun you'll all be blinded.' He added that
'Diamonds are a girl's best friend, so I'm told.' Quick as
a flash Sophie chipped in, 'No, you're my best friend.'

They contentedly answered a flurry of questions.

Asked why they made such a good couple Edward replied lamely, 'I don't know. We just do really.' Sophie, however, was more helpful: 'We share a lot of interests, we laugh a lot and we have a great friendship.' Asked how he proposed, the Prince replied, 'Well, I spoke it.' He was more forthcoming about the wedding itself: 'There is no such thing as a private wedding, but I hope it will be predominantly a family wedding. We chose St George's Chapel because it is a wonderful setting, it is a glorious piece of architecture and it is somewhere slightly different.' He could have added that Sophie had dreamt of her wedding there since the first time she had been to Sunday church with the Queen more than five years before.

For her part Sophie handled herself in the manner of an accomplished, mature woman. She had clearly grown up a lot in five years. Asked how she felt about joining the Royal Family she answered, 'It is slightly nerve-racking in many ways but I am ready for it now. I'm fully aware of the responsibilities and commitments and I think now I am ready.' Edward deflected a question about the failed marriages of his brothers and sisters by observing, 'I think if anybody is going to get married, I hope they think they will get it right. We are the best of friends and we happen to love each other very much and long may that continue.'

The cameras clicked and whirred as Edward placed a gentle kiss on Sophie's cheek. It was Sophie's Kiss and she deserved it.

Other Titles Available from Blake Publishing

Kim Basinger: Longer than Forever
RON BRITTON

> 'When I discovered Richard Gere's secret love letters
> to my wife, I finally understood the truth;
> our passionate ten-year marriage was over.'

Kim Basinger was on the set of her début movie when she met make-up artist Ron Britton. They fell passionately in love, and he became her first husband. Now Ron lifts the lid on one of the world's most desirable women, spilling the beans on her secret affair with Richard Gere, and including scandalous sexy anecdotes and a side of fame that fans are never meant to see.

Hardback £16.99

Johnny Briggs: My Autobiography
JOHNNY BRIGGS

Johnny Briggs' portrayal of *Coronation Street*'s wheeler-dealer Mike Baldwin has made him the man the nation loves to hate. Yet Baldwin's antics pale beside Johnny's real-life roller-coaster ride through more than 50 years of showbusiness.

In this affectionate and immensely readable account of his life, Johnny shows a rare wit as he recalls hilarious escapades with stars old and new.

Hardback £16.99